THE SUPREMACY OF CHRIST

THE PLUMB LINE FROM HEAVEN TO EARTH

Contents

Acknowledgements

I would like to extend thanks to the ones who have helped in the process of this book.

First and foremost to the Father who by the Spirit revealed to me the supremacy of his Son.

My wife, and kingdom partner, Amy. You have prayed for and been patient with me as I have grown in the revelation and relationship with the Supremacy of Christ.

The Spirit inspired authors who were used to impart this revelation into my life. First, the Apostle Paul, who stewarded and suffered for this grand view of Christ. Secondly, Watchman Nee and T. Austin Sparks for their high Christology.

Dr. Don Davis who no matter what I need to talk about brings the focus back upon the supremacy of the Son of God. You are a tuning fork for me as I sing this primary song in the kingdom.

Jesse Allen for writing out my notes and videos into a discernable flow. You did a great job in keeping me working and translating my heart and voice.

Deborah Raney for editing the manuscript. I'm sure 1600 corrections is about average—right?

James W. for the cover and formatting. Your vision and ability in communicating the kingdom is a blessing.

Lastly, I am thankful for all the folks that have prayed and studied with me as I have dove deep into this revelation of the Supremacy of Jesus Christ.

Foreword

I learned recently that my friend and partner in the Gospel, Sam McVay, and I deeply love the same book! I refer to that remarkable text penned years ago by the Chinese teacher and movement leader, Watchman Nee, called Christ: The Sum of All Spiritual Things. The heart of Nee's argument in his tiny book is simple and yet sublime: Jesus of Nazareth is the essence of all spiritual reality. He is not simply the Savior but our very salvation. Jesus is not merely the agent of God who redeems (i.e., the Savior) but the actual salvation he works within and for his creation (i.e., our salvation). In his cryptic language, Nee argued that Jesus is not merely our 'ier" but our 'tion," not merely the Justifier but our justification. He is our all in all: Jesus of Nazareth is supreme.

Sam McVay is an ambassador of Christ who persuasively embodies and declares this supremacy of Christ. From the first meeting we spent together, he highlighted this truth as the core of his emphasis on prayer and revival. Above and beyond all things, Sam articulated, the supremacy of Christ must guide, direct, and infill all efforts in all spiritual activities and ministries. The essence of authentic spirituality and effective ministry is never about that spirituality and ministry per se, i.e., in themselves. Rather, they are paths, means, ways in which we connect to Jesus Christ as our source, sustainer, and end. We do not engage in spiritual efforts and services in Christ's name for any other purpose than the glorification and honor of the only mediator between God and humankind, Jesus of Nazareth.

To be clear on this, God has determined that Jesus should be preeminent in all things. "And he is the head of the body, the church. He is the beginning, the firstborn from the dead, that in everything he might be preeminent. For in him all the fullness of God was pleased to dwell," Col. 1.18-19 (ESV). In the dry language of the theological schools, God wants his Son to have first place in everything: creation, salvation, spirituality, ministry, mission, and anything else related to God and his purpose for the world. Sam articulates and defends this in every walk of his life and ministry. More than once I have been convinced that his continuous focus of Christ's supremacy has allowed him to collaborate with devout believers from every communion and tradition, and places him at the center of a return to an apostolic center that could renew the Church and reboot an anointed effort for global missions focused on restoring Christ's place in spirituality and ministry.

This text (which is the first of a trilogy of works Sam intends to pen on each member of the triune Godhead) will quickly prove to be remarkably helpful in orienting Christ-followers to the basic outline of the biblical argument for the supremacy of Christ in all spirituality and mission. As one of its clearest advocates and most convincing ambassadors, I pray that God will grant his work and ministry the favor it deserves, all to lift up the One whom the Father has granted all his fullness to dwell in bodily form. Truly, Jesus of Nazareth is Lord. Because of that, may we all give him the glory and honor he alone should receive, from all of us, and all of his creation.

Rev. Dr. Don L. Davis

Introduction:

And he is the head of the body, the church; he is the beginning and the firstborn from among the dead, so that in everything he might have the supremacy.
Colossians 1:18 NIV

"On earth as it is in heaven" is the central theme and arguably most known phrase in the Lord's Prayer. Through it Jesus reveals where all of human history is headed and what the earth will be like for all eternity. As in Genesis 1, Heaven precedes the earth. Another way to say it is that the earth is the outward manifestation of heavenly realities. The New Heaven and New Earth spoke of in Revelation 21:1 will be a perfectly harmonized reality filled with the uncontested glory and government of God.

All of the living and "missioning" of Christ's followers should have this view in mind: Heaven is going to fill the entirety of the Earth. The question then is "how can we be sure that our life, family, worship, prayer, house church, or ministry is in agreement with this purpose?" I believe that the only way to guarantee this is to have a correct plumb line so as to guarantee accuracy.

A plumb line is a weight suspended from a string used as a vertical reference line to ensure that a structure is centered. Always finding the vertical axis pointing to the center of gravity, the plumb line ensures everything is right, justified, and centered. Likewise, we need an accurate plumb line so that we are in agreement with what the Lord has determined to build.

So we are left to ask, "What is the accurate plumb line?" I believe it is the Supremacy of Jesus Christ. An accurate and exalted view of Christ is the centering instrument. His preeminence in

Heaven and coming preeminence on Earth are the two great eternal realities.

This book is an effort to set that plumb line in the hearts and minds of today's disciples. We pray that the plumb line be set deep and strong in order to bring the body of Christ into perfect alignment with the prophetic, powerful, and purposeful working of the Holy Spirit in these last days. His Kingdom will come on earth as in heaven, and we can be "plumb-lined" into that purpose by a radical focus upon the Supremacy of Christ.

CHAPTER ONE

Jesus is Supreme

Webster's dictionary states that "supremacy" is the quality or state of having more power or authority than anyone else. Simply put, it's having first place in all things. I am radically committed to the Church's revelation of the supremacy of Jesus Christ. But I am concerned when Bible-teaching churches teach more about the Bible than they teach about Jesus. Don't get me wrong, I am for the Bible. It is the chief witness to the full meal. But it is not the full meal. I am equally concerned that I see charismatic movements teach more about spiritual gifts, signs, and wonders than Jesus. I am for it all: Bible teaching, empowerment of the Holy Spirit, and the manifestation of Heaven on Earth. However, the truths about Jesus can never replace the reality of the Man Christ Jesus. I am convinced that Christ's supremacy being revealed to the Church will weed out of our hearts anything that we have empowered to have supremacy over our lives outside of him. My brothers and sisters, we need an awakening to the reality of how highly enthroned Jesus is over everything. If this happens, we will see the church move in power and purity.

At times I am concerned that the Church becomes more concerned about systems and buildings instead of Christ and His increased Supremacy in our worship and mission. This misplaced concern has allowed us to run the Church by our wits instead of by the power of the Spirit. Discipleship can then be reduced to mental assent to a doctrinal statement and weekly attendance to a meeting. The tragic result of this is that we have made a way of being Christian without knowing Christ. There is a difference between the two, and I pray that this book helps in discerning that.

Popularity not necessarily Supremacy

Jesus being popular doesn't mean, personally and collectively, that he is sitting enthroned as supreme in our lives. A quick look on the internet will reveal that Jesus is the most popular human being to ever live on earth. Since the printing press began operation, approximately 130 million books have been printed. Out of all of these books approximately 40 percent are about Jesus. Time Magazine has declared him as the most famous person in history. Even time is centered on this man's life—it is either B.C. or A.D. If this isn't enough, Jesus is googled approximately 22 million times per month. Jesus is hands down the most popular historical figure in human history.

Jesus is also considered to be the most needed person to ever live. Whether the need is to save them from hell or teach them about solutions to their problems, many go to Jesus to get what they need. But just because he is popular and needed in one's life doesn't make him supreme. In fact, needing him for something in particular could just as well mean that this something is what really reigns supreme in one's life. In the gospels, we read how Jesus was constantly confronting this. As people longed for the miracles of healing, the multiplication of bread, and miracles of various kinds, often what was being revealed was a desire to receive gifts from Jesus as the giver but neglecting Jesus himself as the primary Gift given from God. This is why he constantly confronted humanity about the idolatry in their hearts. Many wanted him for what he could do for them but were blinded that the primary purpose of what he does points to who he is. It is not enough for Jesus to be popular or needed in one's life, he must be supreme in all things, including you.

Throughout this chapter, I will attempt to explain who Jesus Christ is. Each of us is in desperate need of a deeper revelation of the supremacy of Christ. I believe that the Holy Spirit is on a mission to make Jesus supreme in our living, loving, working, etc.

Who is Jesus Christ?

In Matthew 16 Jesus asked the most important question ever and it must be answered by everyone: "Who do you say I am?' He put this question before the disciples, which resulted in a revealing interchange with the Apostle Peter. Peter answered, "You are the Christ, the Son of the living God." At this response, Jesus explained, "Blessed are you, Simon Bar Jonah, for flesh and blood has not revealed this to you, but my Father in heaven." This meant that the answer that Peter gave was a supernatural one. Its source was heaven, not earth.

A closer look at the answer reveals how supernatural it is. The answer had two parts to it. "You are the Christ" and "You are the Son of the Living God." "You are the Christ" means that you are the prophesied man who is the Messiah, i.e. Anointed One. "You are the Son of the Living God" means that you are also literally God. He is THE Son of the Living God. So Peter basically understood that Jesus was an anointed man who was also God. This is the clear answer to the most important question ever asked.

Later the Apostle Paul would write about this glorious answer and expand greatly upon it. This was a stunning miracle since Paul the Apostle was originally Saul the Persecutor, attempting to destroy all things connected to Jesus Christ. Saul, the Pharisee of Pharisees, was convinced that Jesus Christ and this exploding movement of Jesus followers were a blasphemous malignancy that must be removed. But a knocked-off-your-donkey heavenly encounter transformed Paul into one of Christ's most devoted followers.

I like to say that Paul went OCD on Jesus Christ. He didn't just join a movement and decide to attend a service each week. No, Paul went all-in! And this all-in devotion was driven by a glorious and ever growing revelation of who Jesus Christ is. Paul was beaten more, used more, and wrote more than almost anyone in the New Testament. But this was not merely because he had a strong will or some radical devotion. No, these things came from an almost inexpressible revelation of Jesus Christ.

For in him the whole fullness of deity dwells bodily.
Col 2:9

Paul's letters to the churches show how wide and deep was his revelation of Jesus Christ. For example, in the book of Colossians, Paul says, "For in Christ the whole fullness of deity dwells bodily" (Col. 2:9). What a remarkable statement. The fullness of all deity dwelled in this one Jewish man named Jesus Christ. Meaning the omniscient one, omnipotent one, and the one without limit dwelt in a human body. This statement is stunning! It presses the human soul to the precipice of mystery embracing faith.

Jesus is the one who was God in the flesh. It is as vital to know that he is fully God as it is to know that he is fully man. It is as vital to know that he is man as it is to know that he is God. This is the most amazing reality, making him the most unique and incredible man in human history. All other men who have generated followings, such as Muhammad and Buddha, are nothing in comparison to him. They are simply men others are trying to emulate. However, Jesus is the God-Man. This should be savored in your heart and mind, firing you into radical worship.

He is the image of the invisible God.
Col. 1:15

Jesus' manifestation as a man is ultimately expressing the reality that he is the image of the invisible God. The purpose for depicting Christ as "the image of the invisible God" is to describe the correlation between Jesus and Adam. Adam primarily sourced from the Tree of Life in the Garden of Eden. God wanted to have a union with a creature called man and thus manifest his glory everywhere, making known his image. He wasn't going to do this by himself and thus chose Adam and Eve to partner with him in this task.

As a result of Satan's attack, Adam and Eve forfeited sourcing from the life that empowered and enabled them to be the image bearers of Christ's nature. Because of this fall, man became a distorted image that birthed billions of people throughout planet earth who inherited Adam's sin. The manifestation of the image of God, which Adam was meant to be, was distorted, and thus Christ came to be the perfect image. Paul's statement is declaring that Jesus is the ultimate human being. He is the perfect image of what man was meant to be as a representative on behalf of God, reflecting his image.

All things were created through him and for him.

Col. 1:16

Jesus made everything and constructed the dimensions of the galaxies. He constructed the spiritual dimensions and the heart capacity of an angel. He is the owner and heir of everything because everything was made by him. You are alive because Jesus made you for himself. He made you so that he would be satisfied in you and you would be satisfied in him. The purpose of your existence lies within this truth.

If you want a personal purpose and vision statement that is simple, biblical, and placed in reality it is "I was made through Jesus and for Jesus." Once you become calibrated into his Lordship and this revelation, everything else seems so dim in comparison and shifts into proper order. Life will dramatically shift for you when this reality begins to take place and your heart is centered in this truth. Apart from everything else, you were made for Jesus' pleasure. Rev. 4:11 states this truth: "You are worthy, O Lord, to receive glory and honour and power: for you have created all things, and for thy pleasure they are and were created (KJV)." The establishment of his supremacy in our hearts positions us to live a life of great purpose and meaning.

And He is before all things, and in him all things hold together.
  Col. 1:17

Paul declares that Jesus existed before time. Before anything existed there was Jesus. Before one seraphim or cherubim, there was Jesus. Before one star or planet, there was Jesus. Before one ray of light or speck of dust, there was Jesus. If you look at the head of the line of all created things there stands Jesus—the uncreated God. And he is not only before all things, but he is the one holding all things together. At the macro and micro level it is not something but rather someone who is holding all things together. We marvel that as this earth spins at a thousand miles an hour while it is moving around the sun at 67,000 miles per hour you still sit there secure reading while not hurling out into space. Why? Gravity? Well kind of. But the real underlying all unifying and securing reality is not a thing but a Person. The writer of Hebrews will say it this way, "holding all things together by His powerful word" Heb. 1:3. Praise God for the anchor and tether that is Jesus Christ.

He is the head of the body the Church, he is the first born among the dead, so that in everything he may have supremacy.
Col. 1:18 NIV

The crescendo of Christ continues through the pen of Paul. It is a tad of an understatement to say that he has just said a mouthful in the last few verses. But here he shows how deep his OCD runs over this Christ. He is the head of the Body the Church. In other letters we see the glorious view that Paul has of the Church. She is in Christ and thus redeemed, righteous, and will eventually reign over angels and the earth.

The Church is the most powerful organism on the planet. And its head is Christ. Just as the head of a man is the most important part of his body so Christ is at the peak of the Church's vitality. Christ is not only firstborn over all creation but He is also exclusively first in the Church. There is no Body without Him. There is no thought, sight, hearing, or speaking without Him. He is the head, not just some useful appendage. He is where the body will go. He is what the body will do. He is how they will do it. All things come from the head and he most definitely is the Head!

Then he is the firstborn among the dead. This phrase is so unusual it takes some time to process since the whole race of men has been dying since Adam. Isaiah 25 speaks of a veil of death that covers the earth being swallowed up. This was the first gulp. Jesus Christ fully died as a man on the cross. He was dead just like every human before him had been. He was headed for dust when a prophesied divine interruption happened in that tomb. In fact, that tomb became a womb. Mankind is born only from other human wombs. Now something radical had happened. The barren tomb became a fertile womb that birthed the first man to raise from the dead to never die again. In reality the prophesied great global resurrection began two thousand years ago.

The first Man rose to never die again. Soon we will see every tomb that is holding a son or daughter of God also become a womb birthing an eternal never-to-die again body. Jesus is the firstborn from the dead. What a Christ! All of this together leads to one of my favorite phrases and the title of this book. Paul declares that the head-ness of Jesus and the firstborn-ness from the dead of Jesus lead to the truth that Jesus has supremacy in all things. He is preeminent in all things. He deserves to be, is, and will be supreme in all things. His supremacy will reach every nook and cranny of our hearts, the earth, and the ever expanding universe. The Supremacy of Christ is the primary focus and mission of the Holy Spirit on planet earth today. It is the great motivator and unifier of the Body of Christ. The Supremacy of Christ is the plumb-line of all that Jesus is building as He brings heaven to earth. Jesus is Supreme!

We are all personally in desperate need of a supreme revelation of Jesus. The supremacy of Jesus Christ being revealed to a human heart is a supernatural miracle that can only be completed by the work of the Holy Spirit. Though sermons and books serve as a vital part of depicting what the word of God is saying, there is no substitute for the greatest teacher on planet earth, the indwelling Holy Spirit. As we move through this book, I encourage you to dive deep into the Scriptures, asking Jesus for a spirit of wisdom and revelation (Eph. 1:17) so that you may personally know the reality of how high he reigns supreme. This reality was meant to begin in your heart, allowing him first place over all things. In submitting to this truth personally, you will be transformed into what God has designed and destined you for.

Your revelation and submission to the supremacy of Jesus directly correlates with the glory of God you reflect in your life, the testimony of God you give in your life, and the overall health of your Christian life. Jesus is continually probing our hearts asking, "In this moment, am I supreme in your life? Do I sit enthroned upon your affections, your mind, your relationships, your marriage, home, finances, hobbies, etc.? Or, have you allowed what the world offers you to take first place in your life?" Truthfully the Holy Spirit wants to reveal the answer if you simply ask him to. Upon asking him, prepare yourself to embrace the instruction and discipline of the Lord. When we respond to the work of the Spirit with repentance for placing any pleasures of the world above Christ in our lives, we dethrone those lesser lovers and return Christ to his rightful position as the head of every area of our lives.

CHAPTER TWO

Jesus is I Am

I am the Way, the Truth, and the Life…

"So they picked up stones to throw at him…". Jesus elicited strong responses from those he encountered. There seemed to be no middle ground. They either loved him or hated him. In John 8 we have one of the "hate him" moments. Some Jews, religious leaders, were in a conversation with Him about Abraham. One thing led to another and then… Jesus says it, "before Abraham was, I AM!" Response: we must kill the blasphemer who is calling himself God. How did He call himself God, by saying "I AM." In the Bible there are over one hundred Biblical names for God. But the stand alone name is Yahweh. This name actually comes from the encounter that Moses had with God in Exodus 3. When Moses asked, "Who should I say sent me?" His answer is, "tell them that 'I AM WHO I AM'," which was used interchangeably with the sacred and most important name, YAHWEH. Names in the Old Testament revealed the character or unique identity of a person. Eve means 'living." Abraham means Father of great multitude." Moses means "drawn out." Jesus means "saves." So when God resounded to Moses, his use of "I AM" was saying that he transcended all other names. And actually, that he transcends all creation as the Eternal Creator.

Jesus said, "before Abraham was, I am." This was not only a stunning statement about time, that He existed before Abraham. It was also a declaration that He is God! This was the ultimate blasphemy and led to once again, the attempted murder of Jesus.

7 "I am" statements in the book of John

1.) "I am the bread of life." Jn. 6:35,

The situation occurring in John 6 is a progression of Jesus performing signs and wonders to the people. One of the signs Jesus performs is the feeding of the five thousand. After feeding this following, many more begin to flock to him, and his following massively grows. After this happens, Jesus takes his disciples around the lake, leaving behind the growing group of followers. Even though Jesus instructed the crowd to go home, they continue to follow him around the lake. In John 6:26 Jesus says, "Truly, Truly I say to you, you are seeking me not because you saw the signs but because you ate your fill of the loaves." They had moved from amazement that he healed grandma's leg to, "oh my, he can feed our bellies!" In the hierarchy of human needs, providing food was above healing a leg. So there is now an even higher resolve to follow Him. He then says, "Do not work for food that perishes, but for food that endures to eternal life which the Son of Man will give to you for on him God the Father has set his seal" (Jn. 6:27).

This statement cuts the group to the heart, consequently causing them to ask, "What must we do, to be doing the works of God" (Jn. 6:28). Jesus responds, "This is the work of God, that you believe in him whom he has sent." After performing many signs to the people, they continue to be bewildered, asking Jesus what he will do to prove that he is the one whom the Father has sent. They state, "Our fathers ate the manna in the wilderness; as it is written, 'He gave them bread from heaven to eat.' (Jn. 6:31). Essentially they are asking for Jesus to give them bread from heaven as well so that they may live.

Jesus proceeds to engage them by declaring that he is the manna that came down from heaven. It wasn't Moses who fed their ancestors with manna in the wilderness but rather the Father in heaven. In Psalm 78:24-25 David states that this manna from heaven in the wilderness was the bread of angels. This dialogue between Jesus and the crowd is a remarkable heavenly reality that is being revealed. The statement that Jesus is making is that the giving of manna from heaven was a precursor to the provision of the true bread that will be given from heaven which is himself. The following statement would have been hard for anyone to accept. Jesus says, "Eat my flesh and drink my blood" (Jn. 6:53). Jesus had previously alluded to this reality in the statement he made when tempted in the desert, "Man shall not live on bread alone but every word that comes from the mouth of God" (Matt. 4:4). And as we know, the Apostle John writes that Jesus is the Word that became flesh in John 1:14.

After telling them to "eat His flesh and drink His blood," which in the original implies a "one time meal," the crowd begins to be pressed beyond the bounds of natural understanding. But instead of easing their confusion and angst, Jesus then says to them, you must "feed on my flesh" (Jn. 6:54). In Greek this word for "feed" is more active, depicting a process of chewing. This statement, smacking of cannibalism, completely offends the once loyal crowd who turns away en masse and leaves the miracle worker. Just like that—a mega-church gone! Often Jesus leaves us uncomfortable in the words he speaks because he is okay with offending the mind to reveal the heart. And he is radically committed to telling them the truth so that they might eternally live, not just be temporarily satisfied.

While the masses left, the disciples stayed. Jesus questions them saying, "Do you want to go away as well?" (Jn. 6:67) Peter replies in desperation saying, "Lord, to whom shall we go, you have the words of eternal life" (Jn. 6:68). This was a pivotal moment where the twelve became devoted and dedicated disciples. It is as though they are saying, this is a wild ride but you have basically ruined us with your revolutionary words of life. We will never be the same because of you so we will not leave.

Throughout John 6, Jesus is declaring that he is the Word of God that has become flesh and made his dwelling among them. At this point there was not a plethora of Bibles being distributed to everyone. He wasn't offering them a substance that would sustain and strengthen through written words in a human language. No, he was declaring I am the Word of God that gives life. Yes, we want to live by the words of God, but Jesus is stating that I Am the Word of God. Words on a page don't have the ability to transform us from sinners into saints, only Jesus does. The Father has sent the true food and nourishment for every human soul and it is JESUS. True life will not come from your missional accomplishments, being able to do miracles, or even deep doctrines. No, true life will come from your being able to consume Jesus by faith through the Spirit.

2.) "I am the light of the world." Jn. 8:12

Jesus' statement declaring, "I am the light of the world" was connected with the reality of a need for illumination. This crisis for clarity begins at the beginning of time. In Genesis 1, we get a glimpse into the state in which the earth "was formless and void, with darkness over the surface of the deep" (Gen. 1:2). In Genesis 1:3, God spoke to the darkness over the deep saying, "Let there be light, and there was light." What was occurring in this moment was more than a natural phenomena, because the sun wasn't created until the 4th day. The earth was formless and void because of the kingdom of darkness that had been cast down to it (Isa. 14:14-14). It was in Genesis 1 when the light of the Kingdom of God pierced through the domain of the darkness. God was illuminating the darkness of the deep with the light of his Son. This reality continues to this day.

Jesus wasn't declaring in John 8 that the light of his life was occurring for the first time, he was bringing revelation of the reality that has existed forever. Jesus is the light of the world that pierced the darkness of the deep at the beginning of time. The light of Christ is all preaching, meaning everything testifies to this truth. Romans 1:20 states, "For since the creation of the world God's invisible qualities—his eternal power and divine nature—have been clearly seen, being understood from what has been made, so that people are without excuse." Every day the sun rises, illuminating the darkness of the night. Even within this created reality we see the metaphorical depiction of the two spiritual kingdoms that exist.

Jesus saying that he is the "light of life" and whoever follows him will have the light of life (Jn. 8:12) is a statement of illumination that brings revelation of the realities of his identity. It is within this identity, being the light of life, that a revelatory culture is available for all. Meaning Jesus Christ is more than a few revelations in the Bible but rather an ongoing relationship with a light that illuminates you to everything that is life. Think about the sun in the sky, when it shines, it is an essence of itself that is illuminating everything around us. Without the illumination of the sun, the beauty of all that surrounds me (trees, flowers, etc.) becomes an object of distraction that I trip over as I make my way around the darkness rather than a depiction of beauty that I enjoy in the light. We can't even gaze into the sun without becoming impaired. But, it is the sun that illuminates and produces a culture of revelatory insights so that we see truth.

Jesus' miracles are always purposed for illuminating our hearts to see truth in his life. After healing the man born blind, Jesus proceeds to make the following statement, "As long as I am in the world I am the light to the world" (John 9:5). What Jesus did in miracles was revealing what heaven is like, but primarily, it was revealing what he is like. Ultimately heaven is what it is because Jesus is there. The healing of the blind man was a proclamation that Jesus is bringing true illumination and that he is the light of life that pierces through any domain of darkness.

When we have Jesus we have the culture of revelatory insight, having the ability to think and understand truth. Currently this is the opposite reality of the way the world depicts Christianity. Many see Christianity as a mere religion that makes you a bigot filled with pride and arrogance. This can happen within a religious spirit that ends up restricting, consequently cultivating in us an inability to see truth and life within the light of Christ. This then produces a people within the Church who are groping around in the darkness never seeing the realities illuminated by Christ Jesus.

The power of Jesus Christ through the personal presence of the Holy Spirit always brings about a process of illumination so that we can begin to perceive the glories and realities in all that he has made and in all that he is saying (2 Cor. 4:6). This light that penetrates through the presence and power of darkness is made available to all that embrace him.

3.) "I am the door of the sheep." John 10:7,9

The statement that Jesus made in John 10, saying that he is "the door of the sheep" is about the entry into the family of God.

He was declaring that not only is he the "good shepherd" but he is also the door into the pen where the "sheep dwell in safe pasture" (V.9). Jesus is releasing revelation to Israel that he is both the one who watches over God's family and the way into God's family. He is declaring that any other door we attempt to open hoping to enter into a relationship with God will inhibit us from being a part of God's family. By making this declaration that "he is the door of the sheep" Jesus is affirming that he is the Messiah to the Jews and he is the way that the Gentiles enter by his atoning work.

Doors are for entry, but doors are also for locking out the wolves that hunt the sheep. Another reality that Jesus is depicting by declaring he is the door is the protection he provides against any enemies that attempt to destroy the family of God. Jesus says, "The thief comes only to steal and kill and destroy. I came that they may have life and have it abundantly." Jesus is linking this reality to the context of spiritual warfare, that as the door he is both the access point to God and the guardian of the sheep inside God's family. The door here is clearly about guardianship and stewardship over the sheep that come into the pasture of the family of God. As THE door, Jesus stands guard blocking the one who "comes to steal and kill and destroy" (V. 10).

4.) "I am the good shepherd." John 10:11,14

Jesus' "I am" statement in regards to being the "good shepherd" is the fulfillment of the davidic prophetic proclamation of Psalm 23. David proclaimed in Psalms 23 that "The LORD, YAHWEH, is my shepherd." Jesus is clearly stating in John 10 that he is the God of Psalm 23 and that he is a shepherding God. Thus, his leadership and his rule are amazing. He isn't self-centered, focusing on what he can get out of all that his Father has entrusted to him. Rather, his primary focus is on stewarding, protecting, and giving life to the sheep—the children of God's family. His primary mission is empowered by love for his sheep, consequently choosing to lay his own life down for them.

Jesus also depicts himself as a shepherd who speaks to his sheep, interacting with his flock by his voice. He says in verse 16 that the sheep that continue to enter in through him will "listen to his voice." This is revealing the reality that the primary way of interacting with Jesus as his sheep is to listen and obey his voice. Those that don't hear the shepherd's voice are not Jesus' sheep, thus will not follow him (Jn. 10:26-27).

Psalm 23 is an incredible passage full of prophetic promises given to the sheep that are in the pen of the shepherd. Again, Jesus is the fulfillment of these promises given in Psalm 23. It is in him that the realities of what is spoken in this psalm becomes ours. Psalm 23:1 states, "The Lord is my Shepherd, I shall not want." Our soul is knit together to be satisfied in Christ, the Good Shepherd. The world constantly promises us satisfaction. However, what the world yields as a fruit for our soul constantly leaves us wanting more, never satisfying the desires of our heart. In Christ, the longing of our soul is fulfilled and the desires within our heart are satisfied. Jesus is everything we were fashioned to want. In him nothing else is desired.

The anxieties and troubles within this world can quickly devastate our soul. The promise within the pasture of the Good Shepherd is rest, peace, and restoration. Jesus' leadership as a good shepherd is one that lays us down during days of darkness, giving us rest in green pastures (Ps. 23:2). His leadership leads us beside quiet waters amidst the anxiety and worries in life, restoring the strength of our soul (Ps. 23:2-3). It is walking with the good shepherd, Jesus Christ, that leads us down life's path of righteousness to make known the glory of God's ways (Ps. 23:3).

Even though we find ourselves amidst the valleys and shadows of death, in Christ we are free from the fear of what evil can inflict us with. Following Christ as the good shepherd doesn't equate to a life free from struggle but rather a promise of his powerful presence in the midst of it (Ps. 23:4). Submitting to the rod and staff of Jesus' leadership provides the place where comfort in crisis and deliverance in death is attained.

The Good Shepherd prepares a feast in front of the one who attempts to starve our soul of satisfaction (Ps. 23:5). Though we all long for the removal of suffering, it is often within the seasons of suffering where Jesus places his table of abundance in the presence of our enemies. Our good shepherd is the one who anoints us with the oil of gladness in the moments of our greatest despair, overflowing our soul with joy.

5.) "I am the resurrection and the life." John 11:25

In a dialogue with Martha upon the death of Lazarus Jesus declares that he is the resurrection. The eschatological revelation that Jesus is revealing is that he isn't just the resurrector, rather he is the resurrection. While he resurrected people from the dead during his days on earth, ultimately Jesus is expressing his identity as eternal resurrection.

The delay of Jesus' coming at news of the sickness of Lazarus, which ended in his death before Jesus arrived, was actually a purposeful setup for the revealing of himself as the resurrection. At the encounter with Martha, Jesus declares "I am the resurrection and the life" (Jn. 11:25). During this conversation Martha expresses that her hope is set in the reality that Lazarus will rise again on the last day (Jn. 11:24). Essentially Martha is saying that her faith is set doctrinally because there is going to be a global resurrection (1 Cor. 15:23). Jesus presses her, moving her from theological understanding of the reality of resurrection to the present manifestation of resurrection standing before her. By declaring that he "is the resurrection" Jesus is making a statement that resurrection isn't just something that he does, but more accurately is something that he is. He moves Martha's understanding and faith past the fact that he can do something to the reality that he is something, resurrection.

In this dialogue with Martha, Jesus states, "Whoever believes in me, though he die, yet shall he live, and everyone who lives and believes in me shall never die" (Jn. 11:25-26). This is a stunning statement that fully thwarts the power of death. I believe it was from this revelation that Paul gives comfort to those losing loved ones in Christ, saying, "But we do not want you to be uninformed, brothers, about those who are asleep, that you may not grieve as others do who have no hope" (1 Thess. 4:13). It is as if he purposely is stating that his fellow brothers and sisters in Christ do not die. It isn't a denial of biological death but an affirmation that their souls are alive. Paul says, "we would rather be away from the body and at home with the Lord" (2 Cor. 5:8).

This eternal life isn't a place but a person, Jesus Christ. Because of the Holy Spirit given through Christ, we have begun eternal life in the present time. Because of this, death has broken off of us at the spiritual and soul level. Though we biologically die, the essence of our being never perishes.

There will be one generation that doesn't die, but will fly with the Lord upon the appearance of his coming (1 Thess. 4:17). On that day the dead will rise, inheriting their resurrected bodies (1 Thess. 4:16). Because Jesus is the resurrection, those who place their life in Christ will never die.

6.) "I am the true vine." John 15:1, 5

In the series of chapters found in John 13 through 17, Jesus gives glorious revelatory teaching to his disciples. In the middle of these teachings Jesus says, "I am the true vine." He had been teaching them about the Holy Spirit, his resurrection, and never leaving them as orphans. In John 15 he gives a teaching from a common metaphor known to Israel. Often in the Old Testament Israel is referred to as God's vine or vineyard. Jesus takes this metaphor and says to his disciples, "I am the true vine, and my Father is the vine dresser" (Jn. 15:1). As Israel was God's chosen people, being his vineyard of delight, now Jesus is stating that he is the vineyard of his Father's delight. Ultimately Jesus is saying that the Father cannot delight in a people apart from him. Jesus is the delight of God, and in him so are you.

Jesus again states in John 15:5, "I am the vine; you are the branches. Whoever abides in me and I in him, he it is that bears much fruit, for apart from me you can do nothing." Jesus is clearly declaring that he is the place where people are to dwell. We are getting a preview into the revelation that Paul receives of living "in Christ." Jesus is not only going to pay for the sins of the people by doing something for them, he really is going to be the place in which they dwell. David cried out for this place before Christ came to earth, knowing that God's dwelling place is where he would be most satisfied (Ps. 27:4). Jesus is stating that he is the dwelling place that will satisfy the deepest desires of our hearts, empowering us to a life of rich purpose.

Abiding in the vine enables us to take hold of the sap in Christ, the life of the Holy Spirit. It is this life that begins to be the power for bearing fruit. This is a powerful metaphor that Jesus gives to call us to the abiding life. We do not abide in Christianity, doctrine, or mission. We abide solely in the Son of God, Jesus Christ. It is only in the abiding life that we take hold of the abundance in Christ Jesus, being empowered to manifest heaven on earth.

7.) "I am the way, the truth, and the life." John 14:6

      The exclusivity of Jesus' statement is clear and bold. He says "no one comes to the Father except through me" (Jn. 14:6). This statement is clearly depicting the truth that Jesus is not just a great prophet or teacher, but that he is the Messiah, the only way to the Father. There is no way or religion into heaven. Multiple religions present Jesus as a great prophet, miracle worker, or teacher. But this falls far short of the biblical proclamation which makes Jesus the exclusive way for peace with God. There is no neutral ground when it comes to the identity of Jesus. He is very clear that he is the way, the truth, and the life and that apart from him you will never enter into the presence of his Father. His statement demands a clear response, either you are all in or you are all out. There is no middle ground. No one comes to Yahweh or enters into the reality of the covenant of eternal life except through Jesus.

      I want to highlight the inspiration that Watchman Nee has been in my life. His book, "Christ The Sum of All Spiritual Things," revealed to me the truths of Jesus' words in John 14:6. His explanation of this revelation touched my heart, transforming my walk with Christ. It thrust me into a place of savoring Jesus, saying "oh wow he doesn't just give me stuff, he is the stuff." The phrase, "The Father doesn't give us many things, he gives us his Son," rocked my world, bringing to light the reality of what I have in Jesus Christ. For the first time I knew that Jesus was literally the embodiment of way, truth, and life. I realized that all other truths are just descriptions coming out from him and that I do not just get life that comes and goes, but that when I get him I have eternal life.

Jesus didn't come to show you some way, or give you some truths, or give you just life. Jesus is the way, he is truth, and he is life. He doesn't give you an attribute or character trait he carries, he gives you himself. We often separate these things outside of him. As if we can get things from him without actually getting him. There is nothing you can get that is truth and life without solely getting him. The Father does not give us these things through Jesus. He actually gives us all things IN his Son. To say it another way, the Father doesn't give us Things, He gives us His Son. Jesus is Way, Jesus is Truth, and Jesus is Life. When I have Christ I have way, truth, and life. When I have Jesus, I have righteousness, holiness, sanctification (1 Cor. 1:30).

When we attempt to focus on an area of our life that needs refining we are missing the reality that Christianity isn't a matter of behavior modification for our lack of being morally pure. But rather our moral impurity is rooted in our inability to let Christ reign supreme in all things. I could try and articulate in words, ways, truths, and disciplines how to make you better at Christianity. However, it will just be a failure and a frustrating process. What I am laboring for in writing this is for you to more clearly and practically abide in the God-man who has dispensed himself inside of you.

When you get Jesus, you get righteousness, holiness, and sanctification. The process toward a holy Christian life isn't as profound as we have made it to be. Rather it is incredibly simple. Receive Christ, let him reign supreme over all things in your life, and receive all of who he is.

We love gifts from God, but Jesus is not a giver handing out gifts. He is the gift being given by God. Jesus declares He is God through I AM statements and declares that He is then a gift within which are all gifts for those who receive Him. This means our focus is not to be on possessing certain "christian things or virtues."

Our sole focus is to possess the Son of God who is all that we need (Col. 3:11). I primarily want to provoke your soul to feast and savor on Christ through faith.

CHAPTER THREE

Jesus is the True Biblical Hermeneutic

The word hermeneutic describes the interpretive lens that one uses when reading the Scriptures. Jesus truly is the key to interpreting the Scriptures, as he is the purpose and fulfillment of all that is written. When reading Scripture it is essential that we first grasp onto the reality that these are words from God but Jesus is the Word of God. If we miss the reality that in all Scripture Christ is illuminated, much of the interpretation we hold to will be a mere glimpse of the full truth. Jesus alone illuminates the Scriptures and brings revelation of the realities that are spoken throughout all of the Bible.

"You search the Scriptures because you think that in them you have eternal life; and it is they that bear witness about me, yet you refuse to come to me that you may have life."
John 5:39-40

In John chapter 5 Jesus explains that the very thing that the religious leaders of his day were searching for in the Scriptures was standing right before them. As passionate, determined, and zealous as they were to know God through searching the Scriptures, they were unable to see that the truth of everything they studied was written so they would know Jesus. Jesus reveals in this interaction with the Jews that He is the true Biblical Hermeneutic.

It is in this dialogue with the Jew's that Jesus testifies that he is the embodiment of the words of God. In John 5:38 he says, "You do not have his word abiding in you, for you do not believe the one whom he has sent." He is declaring that he is the one who is sent, the abiding word that all Scripture points to. He testifies that he does nothing apart from his Father and everything he does is what the Father is doing. As he continues making these bold declarations he mentions that he isn't the only one who testified about himself. John the Baptist testified the same things about him. The Pharisees were so disgusted by the words that Jesus was declaring, that they began to conspire to kill him.

Jesus' words in John 5:39-40 were primarily releasing revelation that alluded to the reality that the Scriptures the Jews were searching point to everything about his life. While John the Baptist also testifies to this truth, Jesus is stating that the Scriptures they search for life in testify the same. They are so devoted to studying, searching, and knowing what these words say, yet the very one it testifies about they continue to resist and reject. Ultimately Jesus is revealing that the overarching narrative of the Old Testament can be interrupted through his life.

"Did not our hearts burn within us while he talked to us on the road, while he opened to us the Scriptures?"
Luke 24:32

On the road to Emmaus, Jesus explains from Moses through the prophets the Scriptures concerning himself (Lk. 24:27). He explains to these two men that everything that had happened to the Messiah is plainly stated in the Scriptures they know. What they were blinded to without Jesus, in a moment they were enlightened about with him. Not only did the Scriptures make sense, their hearts began to burn with passion and zeal for the revelation Jesus was bringing (Lk. 24:32). As it was with those on the road to Emmaus so it is with us today. The Scriptures are profitable for understanding time, creation, and many scientific realities that point to how the earth was formed. However, the Scriptures' primary purpose is clearly articulating the glory and the revelation of who Jesus is. Jesus alone is the hermeneutic that opens our eyes to see, our ears to hear, and our hearts to receive life. Plainly stated: the Scriptures do not give life, but they rather point to where the life is to be found—Jesus!

Jesus is the one who opens the Scriptures. The word "opened" in the text above has many descriptions in the Greek. From the opening of a womb to one's soul being aroused for greater desire of learning, the way Jesus opens up our hearts is similar. It is in Jesus alone where life can be birthed and one's soul can be aroused to seek and search after him with an unending passion and zeal. Apart from Jesus, the Scriptures are merely a written text book for intellectual information. However with him, the Scriptures become a substance of life that makes our hearts burn, desiring to grow in wisdom and revelation of what is written for the purpose of intimately knowing him.

Jesus Revealed

Jesus is revealed throughout all of the Bible. More so, Jesus is the one who opens the Scriptures in a revelatory way (2 Cor. 3:16). The revealing of Jesus throughout all of Scripture is of utmost importance in our lives. This revelation unveils the Scriptures in such a way that they no longer are a written text of rules but rather a glorious transformative substance that empowers life in us. When

Jesus is unveiled in the Scriptures our eyes are enlightened to know God, his will, and the purposes of our lives (Eph. 1:17-23). Throughout this chapter we are going to uncover some of the ways in which Jesus is revealed throughout the Bible.

In his writings, Paul often uses the word type and shadow to depict that the Old Testament Scriptures, patterns, and traditions are a glimpse into the realities found in Jesus. The word type is a theological word taken directly from the Greek. Paul, in 1 Corinthians 10:11 writes, "These things happened to them as examples and were written down as warnings for us, on whom the fulfillment of the ages has come." The word translated examples here in the NIV is the Greek word tupos, which is literally the word type. Easton's Bible Dictionary defines it as "...a 'model' or 'pattern' or 'mould' into which clay or wax was pressed, that it might take the figure or exact shape of the mould. The word 'type' is generally used to denote a resemblance between something present and something in the future." Therefore, the things of the Old Testament served as a "model" or "pattern" for the things of the New Testament. Throughout the New Testament those things written in the past were considered types.

The word shadow also comes from Paul's writing, one example of which is Colossians 2:16-17 – "Therefore do not let anyone judge you by what you eat or drink, or with regard to a religious festival, a New Moon celebration or a Sabbath day. These are a shadow of the things that were to come; the reality, however, is found in Christ." A shadow is basically the same as a type, in that it represents an Old Testament entity that foreshadows a New Testament truth.

Along with types and shadows there are direct prophecies written about Jesus as well. In the Old Testament alone there are approximately 900-1,000 prophecies concerning Jesus. Approximately 300 of them were fulfilled at his first coming.

Consequently meaning two-thirds of those prophecies are going to be fulfilled upon his final return to earth.

Prophecies are a foretelling of the coming Messiah and details about his life. For example, in Isaiah 53 we are told that he will be "pierced for our transgressions and bruised for our iniquities." This is a clear prophecy of the crucifixion of Christ. We could write dozens of books concerning the prophecies that Jesus fulfilled in his first coming. The accuracy of Jesus' life in fulfilling over 300 prophecies in the Old Testament is astounding.

Jesus is the Key

Jesus is the interpretive key to understanding the whole Old Testament. He is clearly seen in all of Scripture, from the beginning of creation to the prophetic utterances of the coming of a king. Jesus is like a magnifying glass that helps us see clearly and accurately the purpose for the text written throughout the Old Testament. This key, simple as it is, is hidden in plain sight from many people. Without this key, the lock over life will stay latched and the mysteries of the glory of heaven seen in the text of Scripture will continue to be hidden. Jesus is both the key to interpreting the Scriptures and the reward of unlocking the latch. It is in him that the mysteries of wisdom, knowledge, and life written in the Scriptures are found (Col. 2:3).

Jesus, The Key to Creation
And God said, "Let there be light," and there was light.
Gen. 1:3

Jesus is the key to unlock revelation of the power of light seen throughout the Scriptures. In John 8 Jesus says that he is "the light of the world." The light that Jesus radiates wasn't first shone upon his coming to earth. I believe that Jesus was the light that shone through the darkness in Genesis 1:3. We don't see the creation of the sun until day four, yet light exposed darkness on day one. Jesus was before all things and the light of his life is evidenced at the creation of the world. The darkness that hovered over the deep waters of the earth was pierced at the foundations of the world by the light of the Son of God. It was in this moment where the darkness of Satan was exposed and the reality of God's conquering power was seen in the light of his Son.

"In the beginning was the Word, and the Word was with God, and the Word was God. He was in the beginning with God. All things were made through him, and without him was not anything made that was made."
John 1:1-3

Notice that the light of God exposed darkness through spoken word. "God said, let there be light" and the darkness of death fled, releasing life over planet earth. The word that was spoken in Genesis 1:3 released life as it did in John 1. This word wasn't an utterance of a language but the reality of a person. Jesus is the word of God that was dispensed from the mouth of God in Genesis 1, who then became flesh in John 1:14. From the foundations of the earth to the present day, Jesus is the light of mankind that brings life in the midst of death (Eph. 1:4).

And Jesus answered them, "The hour has come for the Son of Man to be glorified. Truly, truly, I say to you, unless a grain of wheat falls into the earth and dies, it remains alone; but if it dies, it bears much fruit."
John 12:23-24

Then on the third day of the creation story, seed was planted in the ground to produce fruit. In John 12 we see Jesus reveal that he is the seed that falls to the ground and dies so that a rich harvest of fruit is produced. There is no coincidence in the Scriptures. Jesus' life is clearly revealing that the story within the Scriptures is constantly depicting him. As the seed fell into the ground on the third day so Jesus was put to death for three days before being resurrected as the tree of life that produces eternal fruit. Jesus is the ultimate seed to humanity that produces life within us that bears rich fruit.

Then God said, "Let us make man in our image, after our likeness. And let them have dominion over the fish of the sea and over the birds of the heavens and over the livestock and over all the earth and over every creeping thing that creeps on the earth."
Gen. 1:26

Jesus again clearly is being depicted on the sixth day at the creation of mankind when Adam was formed as an image bearer of God. Adam was a representative of God in both image and authority. It was on the sixth day that God gave Adam authority over the earth. God blessed Adam by placing him in the Garden of Eden to walk in his presence. He commissioned him to fill the earth with the glory of God, giving him authority to put underfoot everything that would set itself up against God's intimate knowledge increasing throughout the world (Gen. 1:28). As gracious of a gift as God gave Adam in bearing his image and walking in his authority, he was merely a foreshadow of Jesus.

He is the image of the invisible God, the firstborn of all creation.
Col. 1:15

Before the foundations of the world Jesus was predestined to be the perfect human that bore the image of God (Col. 1:17, Rom. 8:29, Eph. 1:4). He was destined to inherit the full dominion to subdue both heaven and earth. The commission given Adam to multiply, increase, and fill the earth is perfectly fulfilled in Christ. To this day, Jesus continues to put underfoot all that set itself up against the increase of God's Kingdom across planet earth (1 Cor. 15:24-25). Jesus is the perfect image of God carrying his authority over heaven and earth (2 Cor. 4:4,6, Matt. 28:18). Again, Jesus reveals the purposes of God seen in the creation story on day six. It is in him, through him, and for him that all is written in the Scriptures and created on the earth (Col. 1:16). Jesus became the final and perfect Adam to redeem and rescue the human race from Adam's seed of death, imparting his seed of life (1 Cor. 15:22,45).

Therefore a man shall leave his father and his mother and hold fast to his wife, and they shall become one flesh.
Gen. 2:24

As Adam was a foreshadow of Jesus, Eve was a foreshadow of the Church. The gospel story is clearly prophesied in the creation of Eve and the prophetic utterance of marriage in Genesis 2. Genesis 2:21 states, "So the Lord God caused a deep sleep to fall upon the man, and while he slept took one of his ribs and closed up its place with flesh. And the rib that the Lord God had taken from the man he made into a woman and brought her to the man." As Adam was laid to rest for the life of Eve, so Jesus was laid to rest for the life of the Church. As Eve was created from Adam's side, so we are given life from the piercing of Christ's side (Is. 53:5). John 19:33-34 states, "But when they came to Jesus and saw that he was already dead, they did not break his legs. But one of the soldiers pierced his side with a spear, and at once there came out blood and water." The life of Eve given through Adam is a foreshadow of the life of the Church given through Christ. The fact that the creation of Eve's life foreshadows the life of the Church is remarkable. At the creation of the world Jesus is clearly depicted as the savior of a new humanity.

"This mystery is profound, and I am saying that it refers to Christ and the church."
Eph. 5:32

The awe of all Scripture pointing to Christ and his Church from the beginning of time continues. In Genesis 2:24 we see a prophetic utterance of a future marriage. It states, "Therefore a man shall leave his father and his mother and hold fast to his wife, and they shall become one flesh." This statement can't yet be seen in humanity as Adam and Eve weren't formed from the womb of a woman. There was no father or mother for them to leave to be united as one flesh. Paul brings revelation to this statement in Ephesians when he says, "This mystery is profound, and I am saying that it refers to Christ and the church" (Eph. 5:32). This statement in Genesis 2 is a foreshadow of Jesus leaving his Father in Heaven to be united with his wife on earth. Jesus' first coming united us with him as one in spirit (1 Cor. 6:17), but it is at his next coming that the marriage supper and unification of what is prophesied in Genesis 2 will be fully fulfilled. It is then that we will be one with him in flesh, fully married as his Bride.

Then the eyes of both were opened, and they knew that they were
naked. And they sewed fig leaves together and made themselves
loincloths.
  Gen. 3:7

Throughout the first three chapters of Genesis we see the foreshadowings of Jesus everywhere. We see him depicted in the creation, purpose, and also redemption of humanity. It was at the fall that Adam and Eve recognized their vulnerability of being fully exposed. It was at their disobedience that their eyes were taken off of God and placed on themselves. It was in this moment where works birthed from the flesh began and they sewed together fig leaves to cover themselves. These fig leaves represented human based works to cover up a lack of faith, obedience, and love for God. This moment began the necessity of God's redeeming love to clothe and cover the sin and disobedience of humanity.

And the Lord God made for Adam and for his wife garments of skins
and clothed them.
Gen. 3:21

Immediately we see the nature of God's love and grace over humanity as he clothes them with garments of animal skin in place of their fleshly fig leaves. This is another prophetic foreshadow of the perfect lamb who will be slain to clothe humanity in full righteousness and holiness. Jesus is the lamb who was slain to clothe us even as animal skins replaced the works of Adam's and Eve's fig leaves. From the fall, we can see the future fulfillment of the finished work of God as he slays the perfect lamb for the redemptive clothing of humanity.

Jesus, the Great Hero of Faith

Jesus, the pioneer and perfecter of faith.
Heb. 12:2

Throughout all of the Old Testament we have heroes who lived by faith, fixing their eyes on the future fulfillment that Christ would bring. All of these people, as heroic as they were, were types and foreshadows of the coming forerunner who would bring to fruition all that God has prepared for humanity. Jesus is our great hero of faith who ran ahead of us to fulfill all that was seen in God's people throughout the Old Testament.

Noah

For as were the days of Noah, so will be the coming of the Son of Man.
Matt. 24:37

Noah's life was a foreshadow of Jesus, depicting a man who by faith would labor and toil in pain preparing a place for humanity to be spared from the wrath of God. Jesus is the true Ark that we enter into to escape destruction. As it was in the days of Noah, so it will be in the coming day of the Son of Man (Matt. 24:37). As God cleared the wicked rebellion of the people from earth in the days of Noah, so he will clear it again upon Jesus' second coming as King.

The ark entered into by faith is found in Christ, protecting us against the coming wrath of God as he judges the world for its wicked rebellion (Col. 3:6, Rev. 19:15). As Noah entered into the ark by faith so we enter into the ark of heaven by faith, hidden away with Christ in God (Col. 3:3). It is in Christ alone that we are sealed, saved, and delivered from the coming pains of death as God clears the earth of all its wickedness.

Abraham

The promises were spoken to Abraham and to his seed. Scripture does not say "and to seeds," meaning many people, but "and to your seed," meaning one person, who is Christ.
- Gal. 3:16

     Abraham was a type of Christ foreshadowing the salvation that would occur through faith for Jews and Gentiles (Gal. 3:8). Abraham obeyed God in faith going to a foreign land to prepare a nation that God would bless and descend his Son from. The seed of salvation that God promised Abraham and his descendants came through Jesus (Gen. 22:18, Gal. 3:16). Jesus is the true seed from Abraham that blesses the nations. It is in the seed of Christ that we are Abraham's offspring, receiving through faith the promise of being heirs of God (Gal. 3:29).

Isaac

"Take your son, your only son Isaac, whom you love, and offer him there as a burnt offering on one of the mountains."
Gen. 22:2

For God so loved the world, that he gave his only Son.
John 3:16

     Abraham was given a miracle child, Isaac, through a promise spoken by God. As Isaac was given as a promised son, so was Jesus given to the world. Jesus is the perfect representation of Isaac's birth and also the fulfillment of him as a sacrificed son. Isaac was spared the pain of being sacrificed on the altar, Jesus was not. Isaac was a foreshadow of Christ being sacrificed by his Father on the altar of the cross. Jesus is the perfect sacrificed son, having his blood shed for our sins and his body broken for our healing (Is. 53:5, Heb. 9:22, 1 Pet. 2:24).

Moses

Moses was a representative on God's behalf as a servant, but Jesus was his representative as a son (Heb. 3:5-6). As Moses delivered the Israelites from the grasp of Egypt's rule, so Jesus delivered humanity from the grasp of Satan's rule. Jesus is the fulfillment of what Moses spoke to regarding what God would do in the future. Moses was a foreshadow of Jesus, as Jesus is the perfect representative of the God who brought deliverance from the devil's slavery of death.

Jesus is the Temple Fulfillment

The temple that was built by human hands was a mere foreshadow of the temple built by God's hands. God's heart was never that humanity would build the temple in which he dwelt but that they would be the temple in which he dwelled (Acts 17:24). As the temple was a temporary place where the presence of God dwelled, Jesus is the fulfillment of the eternal place in which his presence dwells. Jesus' body is the temple destroyed and rebuilt by God's power, enabling humanity to continually remain in the presence of God (Jn. 2:21).

David

He will reign on David's throne and over his kingdom.

Isa. 9:7

David was the anointed king destined to reign and rule with justice and righteousness over the nation of Israel. However he was a foreshadow of the Anointed King of God, Jesus Christ, who will reign and rule with justice and righteousness across the world. Jesus is the coming king to rule all nations, and through his leadership increase the government and peace of God across the earth.

The Heir to the Inheritance

"Ask me, and I will make the nations your inheritance, the ends of the earth your possession."

Psalm 2:8

As God's son, Christ is the heir to the inheritance that is prophesied throughout all the Old Testament. Jesus Christ is the one who is promised to not see decay through death but rather inherit life (Ps. 16:10). Christ is the one who will inherit the nations of the earth, reigning and ruling across the world as king.

Jesus Prophesied in Isaiah

Jesus is the man born of a virgin woman as the promised Messiah to the world (Is. 7:14). He is the one who is prophesied to suffer death and be propelled into heaven as God's glorious Son (Is. 53:10-12). Jesus is the present and future fulfillment of a God called "Wonderful Counselor, Mighty God, Everlasting Father, Prince of Peace." (Is. 9:6). Jesus is the conquering king who will return to the earth to judge and dismantle the wicked rebellion from the world (Is. 63:2-6).

Jesus is the Son of Man

"I looked, and there before me was one like a son of man, coming with the clouds of heaven."
Daniel 7:13

The Son of Man that Daniel saw in his vision coming with the clouds of heaven was Christ. Jesus is the suffering servant, made glorious son, who is coming to earth a second time when he pierces the eastern gate of the sky as king (Dan. 7:14, Matt. 24:27). Jesus is the prophesied son who will receive the praise and exaltation of the people of the earth as he takes authority over the world (Dan. 7:14, Matt. 28:18).

CHAPTER FOUR

Jesus: The Promised Messiah

Of all the promises and prophecies given to Israel, the centerpiece of them all were the ones about the coming Messiah. From the book of Genesis through Malachi the Lord whispered—and shouted—the reality that a Jewish Messiah would be manifested to liberate Israel and to set up a global eternal kingdom. These promises and prophecies have ramifications for the Jews, Gentiles, and the whole kingdom of darkness.

In his Encyclopedia of Biblical Prophecy, J. Barton Payne itemized 127 Messianic predictions involving more than 3,000 Bible verses, with a remarkable 574 verses referring directly to a personal Messiah! The word "Messiah" or "Anointed One" (or in Greek, "Christ"), is taken from Psalm 2:2 and Daniel 9:25-26.

Walter C. Kaiser Jr, The Messiah in the Old Testament
<u>Here are some of the definite clues about this coming that God gave in the Old Testament:</u>

- The Messiah would be the seed/offspring of a woman and would crush the head of Satan (Genesis 3:15).
- He would come from the seed/offspring of Abraham and would bless all the nations on earth (Genesis 12:3).
- He would be a "prophet like Moses" to whom God said we must listen (Deuteronomy 18:15).

- He would be born in Bethlehem of Judah (Micah 5:2).
- He would be born of a virgin (Isaiah 7:14).
- He would have a throne, a kingdom and a dynasty, or house, starting with King David, that will last forever (2 Samuel 7:16).
- He would be called "Wonderful Counselor," "Mighty God," "Everlasting Father," "Prince of Peace," and would possess an everlasting kingdom (Isaiah 9:6-7).
- He would ride into Jerusalem on a donkey, righteous and having salvation, coming with gentleness (Zechariah 9:9-10).
- He would be pierced for our transgression and crushed for our iniquities (Isaiah 53:5).
- He would die among the wicked ones but be buried with the rich (Isaiah 53:9).
- He would be resurrected from the grave, for God would not allow His Holy One to suffer decay (Psalm 16:10).
- He would come again from the clouds of heaven as the Son of Man (Daniel 7:13-14).
- He would be the "Sun of Righteousness" for all who revere Him and look for His coming again (Malachi 4:2).
- He is the One whom Israel will one day recognize as the One they pierced, causing bitter grief (Zechariah 12:10).

All of these "prophetic clues" have been and will be fulfilled in Jesus The Messiah.

Messiah—Supernaturally Born

The promised and prophesied birth of Jesus is astounding. Approximately 700 years before the birth of Jesus, Isaiah prophesied that a coming Messiah would be born of a virgin woman. Isaiah declared that this supernatural birth would be a sign to Israel that their God was among them (Is. 7:14). This incredibly accurate prophecy of Isaiah was what God promised thousands of years prior, that a man would be born who would be anointed to crush humanity's enemies under their feet, delivering them from their sins and from the destruction of Satan (Gen 3:15).

In chapter one of both Matthew and Luke is recorded the fulfillment of this prophetic promise. The chosen carrier of the promised and prophesied savior of the world was Mary, a virgin teenage girl, favored by God to carry his Son and give birth to the promised Messiah. An angel appeared to Mary stating that the conception of this child would come by the presence of the Holy Spirit as she was overshadowed by God's power (Lk. 1:35).

This supernatural conception was again confirmed as an angel appeared to Joseph, Mary's fiancé, declaring that the baby conceived in the womb of his wife was the Son of God, born not of natural, but of heavenly descent (Matt. 1:20). Both the conception and the birth of Jesus Christ confirmed the prophetic word of Isaiah fulfilling the promise of God (Matt. 1:23).

Not only was Jesus supernaturally conceived, but stunningly enough, he was chosen to be carried by one who was culturally despised and thought foolish. Both Mary and Joseph held no esteem in the eyes of humanity. This supernatural conception and birth again demonstrated the wisdom of God that is foolish in the eyes of human wisdom. In every aspect, Jesus' birth is the most unique and supernatural birth in human history.

Messiah—Supernatural Ministry

Jesus' ministry was equally as supernatural as his birth. Though he lived 33 years, his ministry of powerful proclamation and demonstration of the Kingdom of God was only exhibited the last three years of his life. The way for his ministry was prepared by John the Baptist who was calling people to repentance for their sins. The baptism that John gave was qualified by the sinful nature of humanity. Jesus, perfect though he was, came to John to be baptized. He was disqualified for this baptism because he was one who was perfect in nature, needing no repentance for sin. It was at his obedience to participate in what he wasn't qualified for that power came.

As Jesus arose from the water, the heavens split open and the Holy Spirit descended on him like a dove, in bodily form (Lk. 3:22). This is a pivotal point in Jesus' life as the trajectory of what he does dramatically shifts after this. Jesus' baptism was not one of repentance but of the Holy Spirit. Though transformation into a new nature was not needed for his next season of life, an impartation from heaven was. As righteous as Jesus was, he needed more than Godly behavior, he needed his Father's power. It was at this moment that Jesus was anointed by the Holy Spirit to execute his Father's commands by proclaiming with authority and demonstrating in power the Kingdom of God (Lk. 4:18-19). The presence of the Holy Spirit was what propelled Jesus into powerful ministry.

Jesus' ministry was not for the purpose of starting a religion called Christianity but for bringing the Kingdom of God to earth. Simply put, the Kingdom of God is the dominion in which Jesus sits enthroned as king. Jesus began his ministry by proclaiming this truth and drawing humanity into relationship with him through repentance (Matt. 4:17). Jesus did not merely articulate the Kingdom of God through wise rhetoric but with authoritative proclamation. This was evidenced as the people recognized that Jesus carried something different than the teachers of the law. The distinguishing mark was that Jesus taught with authority; the teachers of the law didn't (Matt. 7:29). The proclamation that Jesus made was powerful as it pierced past human wisdom and released the presence of God. Jesus' authority empowered his words to take intellectual information taught by the teachers of the law and make those words a powerful impartation into people's hearts.

Jesus' three and a half year ministry was also accompanied by remarkable power as he performed signs, wonders, and miracles never seen before. Jesus was doing more than just performing miracles, he was demonstrating the realities of his dominion. Jesus commissioned his disciples in Matthew 10:7 to "Go proclaim that the Kingdom of Heaven is at hand." He then commanded them to demonstrate the reality of what they proclaimed by "Healing the sick, raising the dead, cleansing the lepers, and casting out demons" (Matt. 10:8). Because diseases, death, and demons don't exist in heaven, Jesus was demonstrating that when the Kingdom of Heaven draws near, that which exists there manifests here.

Both Jesus' unusual authority of teaching and power in performing signs, wonders, and miracles confirmed his identity as the promised Messiah.

Messiah Crucified

The culmination of Jesus' powerful ministry was one of rejection from his followers and betrayal from his disciple Judas. As his supernatural birth was promised and prophesied, so was his gruesome death. The rejection and rebellion against God's Anointed, as the Pharisees and political leaders of Rome conspired together against Jesus' Lordship, was prophesied in Psalm 2:1-2. The death of Jesus was always the plan and pathway for humanity to be restored to their intended state (Is. 53:10). Isaiah 22:23-25 prophesied that the messianic deliverer would be driven like a peg into a firm place taking on the load of his offspring. Jesus' season of suffering was also prophesied in Ps. 22 declaring that he would be mocked, despised, and pierced by the peoples of the earth. Isaiah 53 again prophesied that the promised Messiah would come as a man who had no form of beauty but was beheld by God as his Son.

Jesus' powerful ministry was a foretaste of the Kingdom of God as his primary mission was not to perform miracles or reveal Scripture but to defeat death and bring life. Though the people wanted a king who would rule by force, his coming as a suffering servant set humanity free from slavery and brought it into sonship by adoption (Rom. 8:15). Humanity's entry into the Kingdom that Jesus preached and demonstrated came through his crucifixion at the cross. Though Jesus could have ruled as king over slaves, his crucifixion was the act of sacrificial obedience that enabled him to get what he most desired—you!

Jesus agonized on the cross for six hours as he died for the sins of the world. Jesus is the Messiah liberating humanity from their sin. This gruesome act of death that should have led to a guilty sentence against Jesus' accusers, became the most glorious act of grace that led to a sentence of innocence and freedom. What the enemy intended for the demise of Jesus became humanity's deliverance and the devil's destruction.

Jesus' crucifixion was no mere martyrdom, he was an innocent man doing an anointed messianic work of marching on sin by becoming sin for us (2 Cor. 5:21). At the beginning of man's rebellion God promised that this destruction of Satan would occur as Jesus crushes the head of the serpent (Gen. 3:15). Shockingly though, Jesus took on the very sentence Satan had against humanity, delivering us from the depths of death.

Messiah Resurrected

As Jesus' crucifixion was always the plan that was promised and prophesied, so was his resurrection. Throughout the Old Testament we see these prophetic utterances speaking of a son who would be resurrected, not being left in the decay of death. Psalm 16:10 prophetically speaks into the coming resurrection of the Messiah saying, "For you will not abandon my soul to Sheol, or let your holy one see corruption." The holy one that has not been held captive by corruption or abandoned in the depths of death is Jesus, the promised Messiah.

"He shall build a house for my name, and I will establish the throne of his kingdom forever."
2 Sam. 7:13

There are many places in the Scriptures where "forever throne" is the descriptive declaration of what God promises to do in the future. This throne is not merely occupied in temporary time by a man wearing the body of Adam. Though a foretaste of this promised throne was seen in David's offspring, Solomon, it was not the fulfillment of this prophetic promise. The throne that Solomon sat on and the temple he built were temporary. This declaration given by Nathan was prophesying of the coming days of the promised Messiah.

This promise wasn't fulfilled during the days of Jesus living on earth two thousand years ago. It wasn't in his mortal body that this promised Messiah would be established forever, but in his resurrected eternal body. Jesus did not see the decay of death in the depths of Sheol. He was raised to life, inheriting a new eternal body in which to reign and rule on the prophesied throne of his kingdom. Jesus' crucifixion legally erases in present and eternal time the accusations and sentences of Satan. His resurrection empowers us to hold onto hope, in faith believing that our mortal death is the pathway to receiving our resurrected bodies forever (Rom 8:23-25). Jesus is the firstfruits of resurrection as those who

54

place their faith and hope in him will receive their prophesied and promised resurrected body for eternity (Rom. 8:29. Col. 1:18).

Messiah—Ascended

After Jesus' resurrection he spent forty days among the disciples giving proof to his resurrection and teaching them about the Kingdom of God (Acts 1:3). After these forty days Jesus ascended into the clouds of heaven right before the disciples' eyes (Acts 1:9). He didn't disappear, vanishing away in the clouds. Jesus ascended to the right hand of his Father in heaven to occupy his promised throne in his resurrected body (Acts 2:33). Jesus' ascension to be exalted at the right hand of his Father is remarkable as he is currently seated in power above all things (Eph. 1:21, Heb. 1:4).

After being baptized by the Holy Spirit, Peter declares that Jesus has received the promised Holy Spirit and is now pouring it out upon humanity (Acts 2:33). Not only is Jesus freely pouring out his Spirit of life, but as the Messiah he is transformingly reigning and ruling over all things as the Lord and Christ. Jesus' crucifixion, resurrection, and ascension is the blueprint for sitting underneath his leadership as Lord and being set free into a life of holiness, righteousness, and redemption (Rom. 8:34. 1 Cor. 1:30).

The glory of Jesus' messianic reign has begun already as he is establishing his kingdom over every power, authority, and dominion that sets itself up against God (1 Cor. 15:24). The reality of Jesus' reign is more eternally real than anything you temporarily see. He is currently sitting at the right hand of the Father with hair as white as wool, eyes like blazing fire, feet burning like bronze, a voice that sounds like rushing waters, with a face that shines like the sun in all of its brilliance (Rev. 1:14-17). We aren't waiting for Jesus' reign to begin, it has begun in the heavenly realms. If this reality isn't stunning enough, we have access to the throne room of this man's reign to gaze by faith at his beauty and glory in his resurrected body (Heb. 4:16). When we gaze at his glory we become begotten by God and transformed into Christ's image (1 Jn. 3:2, 1 Cor. 3:17-18). It is by beholding him in his resurrected body that we become like him in this world (1 Jn. 4:17).

Messiah Coming Again

Jesus' current reign in the heavenly realms will manifest as his glory fully invades earth. Christ's return will fulfill the mystery of God that has been preached and proclaimed for the last two thousand years. When he returns, this mystery that is currently manifested in the spirit of man will be fully manifested as he brings together all things of heaven and earth in perfect unity, establishing his throne on earth forever (Eph. 1:9-10). The bringing of heaven and earth together will occur under the Messianic lordship of Jesus, which is the coming again of Jesus Christ.

Jesus' return to earth isn't a mythology or metaphorical picture. The Bible clearly depicts the coming again of Jesus Christ, declaring that he will come as a conquering king not a suffering servant. When the seventh trumpet blows at the end of this age, the Son of Man will come with the clouds of heaven as he pierces the eastern gate of the sky, ushering in his Kingdom across planet earth (Dan. 7:13-14, Matt. 24: 27, Rev. 11:15). It is at his second coming where we are made fully like him in all his glory (1 Jn. 3:2, Col. 3:4). In a flash, in a twinkling of an eye, at the sound of the last trumpet, the dead will be raised and those living on earth will be changed as we are caught up in the clouds riding behind Jesus as he establishes his reign over everything (1 Cor. 15:51-52, Rev. 19:14).

The most climatic moment in human history will occur at the culmination of this age as Jesus returns to earth. Everything we do is meant to be purposed for this day. Whether regarding our prayer, mission, or everyday life, our fixation on this future fulfillment hastens the wedding supper of the lamb and the union of Jesus and his bride (Is. 62:5, 2 Pet. 3:12, Rev. 19:7-8). The cross of Christ was our engagement with Jesus not our wedding day. This is a critical revelation that we all need, as the greatest day of our lives has yet to occur. As a bride passionately prepares and anxiously awaits her union with her husband, so do we await our union with Christ. The blessed hope that we passionately prepare for and anxiously await is the glorious coming of our Lord and Savior Jesus Christ (Titus 2:13). Our preparation and participation occurs as we persistently ask God the Father for the release of his Son's reign (Rev. 22:17). The Lord's prayer, "Your Kingdom come and your will be done on earth as it is in heaven" will be fully manifested at the second coming of the promised Messiah.

CHAPTER FIVE

The Builder and the Bridegroom of the Church

The Church has expanded from a ragtag rejected small group of twelve and has turned into a catalyst of hope with a couple billion people on planet earth. This type of movement cannot be built through human wisdom, strategy, or strength. This reality of the greatest movement in human history testifies to the truth that Jesus is the builder of the Church and the bridegroom who woos humanity to himself.

The Church is the most blessed and powerful people on planet earth. An increasing revelation of the beauty and power of God's bride, the Church, is needed if we are to partner with Christ to fulfill our mandate as his people. The Church's primary purpose in mission is to be a blessing to the nations, as was promised to Abram in Genesis 12. The Church is not just another sociological institution. In fact, without the Church the nations would have committed global suicide by now. The Church is an eternal family, a living organism, and the only hope for a lost world. The Church is the chosen catalyst in this age to carry and release the presence and power of heaven to the earth, bringing about the eternal reign of Jesus Christ.

However, the Church can't carry its purpose without fully knowing and submitting to the person who builds and betroths her. Jesus came to earth to both build and betroth his bride, the Church.

This bride is not merely many individuals but a corporate body of believers. What Jesus came to build was a body who would abide in him, thus becoming a unified bride that offered herself together as a reward for his suffering. As Eve came out of Adam so the Church comes out of Jesus. The Church cannot carry its identity or purpose unless it is solely connected with her husband, Jesus Christ. The Church is both birthed through and will be forever married to Christ. When these two realities are lived into, the supremacy of Jesus is manifested on earth as it is in heaven. Our surrender to Jesus' leadership as builder and active union with him as husband empowers us to co-labor with him to reign and rule forever.

The supremacy of Jesus is not merely a theological topic of discussion but a spiritual reality that we choose to, or not to, participate in by faith. Where the church actively chooses to seat Jesus will determine how we move forward with him as both builder and bridegroom. Jesus must be placed first in everything that we do as the church. If not, we will build the church with systems that we marry in the name of Jesus that are not him.

The Builder of the Church

What is remarkable is that Jesus was predestined to be the builder of the Church before the foundations of the earth. He was predestined to build back what would be broken in humanity to its original intention, being a people sustained and strengthened by God. The eternal counsels of heaven had determined before the formation of the earth that Jesus would be the one who would build the Church through buying her back into the family of God (Eph. 1:4). The Church can exist and function only because Jesus is supreme above all things. It is through his death that he began to build the Church through delivering her from the grasps of the devil. Without the enthronement of Jesus as King, humanity can never be built into God's people, the Church.

When Jesus came to the region of Caesarea Philippi, he asked his
disciples, "Who do people say the Son of Man is?"
- Matt. 16:13

Knowing the context in which Jesus spoke his words holds critical significance that sheds greater light and insight into what he was speaking. In the context of this passage, Jesus was standing on the foothills of the region of Caesarea Philippi, a city set on a hill that culturally resembled Las Vegas. Just below this wicked city sat a visible open mouth that was called the gates of Hades. At the time this literal location was considered an open portal to the demonic underworld.

Looking upon this city and the mouth of the gates of Hades, Jesus engages his disciples by asking them the most important question in human history, "Who do people say the Son of Man is?" The Son of Man was Jesus' most commonly used title to declare who he was, stating it 78 times throughout the four gospels. In the context of this day, whenever Jesus taught he often was referring to Old Testament passages that his audience knew he was drawing from. In this instance his disciples knew he was referring to Daniel's prophetic vision: "I saw in the night visions, and behold, with the clouds of heaven there came one like a son of man, and he came to the Ancient of Days and was presented before him. And to him was given dominion and glory and a kingdom, that all peoples, nations, and languages should serve him; his dominion is an everlasting dominion, which shall not pass away, and his kingdom one that shall not be destroyed." (Dan. 7:13).

This is one of the most significant visions recorded in all of the Old Testament. Daniel himself is stunned by the vision saying, "There came one riding on the clouds like the son of man." In the Scriptures it is only Yahweh God who rides upon the clouds. "Bless the Lord, O my soul! O Lord my God, You are very great! You are clothed with splendor and majesty, covering yourself with light as with a garment, stretching out the heavens like a tent. He lays the beams of his chambers on the waters; he makes the clouds his chariot; he rides on the wings of the wind" (Ps. 104:1-3). Daniel's vision was depicting that the son of man who rides on the clouds of heaven is a divine man who is God. The divine man Daniel saw was given all authority to execute an everlasting kingdom. Jesus was referring to Daniel 7:13 when he declared in Matthew 28:18, "All authority in heaven and earth has been given to me." Essentially Jesus is saying that he is the Son of Man Daniel envisioned riding on the clouds of heaven and authoritatively enacting an everlasting kingdom across the earth. This revelation of the gospel of the kingdom was proclaimed by John the Baptist, Jesus, and the apostles. We now are commissioned to preach and proclaim the same gospel of the kingdom for the purpose of ushering in the return of Jesus (Matt. 24:14).

His disciples knew the hope that Israel had, stated in Daniel, in this coming Son of Man who will conquer the entire world as king forever. In asking them, "Who do people say the Son of Man is?" He is directly referencing the reality of what Daniel prophesied. Jesus asking this question and referring to himself as this man is stunning. He is declaring that the hope of Israel's conquering king that is given all dominion, glory, and praise is him. Ultimately he is saying that the authority that the son of man was given in the text in Daniel is going to be given to him to build the Church.

The national deliverance from oppression that Israel longed for would be accomplished by what they understood as the primary mission of the prophesied Messiah. Jesus' desire to keep hidden his title as Messiah and rather, to link himself to the Son of Man was important to him and so it should be understood by us. Jesus declaring himself as Messiah in the context of his day was declaring that he would be the national deliverer that would set Israel free from the oppression of Rome. In the days of Jesus many had come proclaiming to be a "messiah" that would deliver people from national oppression. Israel primarily longed for this national deliverance, and if Jesus would have declared himself as Messiah, it is likely that the public crowds along with the Jewish counsel would have devised a plan with this man to overtake Rome. Though Jesus knew he was the Messiah, he also knew that his messianic mission to deliver humanity from their national oppression wasn't occurring at his first coming, but at his second.

This is why Jesus' favorite phrase to identify himself was as the Son of Man. Being the Son of Man wasn't declaring what he would do but who he is. By stating he is the Son of Man he was declaring his identity as the divine man descended from heaven as God in the flesh. The reason Jesus linked himself to this title was because he deeply desired relationship and thus desired for his identity to be made known so that humanity would draw near to God through him. Though he could build his government across the world without us, he won't. His first desire is to build his Church through a people who have revelation of his identity so that they can partner with him to extend his government across planet earth as he ushers in as Messiah of the world at his second coming.

The simplicity of this question—"Who do people say the Son of Man is?"—holds profound implications for our lives. It is stunning that the system by which Jesus builds his Church isn't through enforcing his power and authority. While Jesus could have built his body at the hands of subjecting his disciples to his God-given authority, he chose to release control and empower humanity to choose by faith to believe in him. This faith begins by answering the most important question in human history, "Who do you say the Son of Man is?" The response to this question has dramatic implications for our lives. As Jesus asked his disciples two thousand years ago, he continues to build his Church today by asking the same question.

They replied, "Some say John the Baptist; others say Elijah; and still others, Jeremiah or one of the prophets."
 Matt. 16:14

The disciples responded by stating what the word on the street was. They were declaring that others believed that Jesus, as the Son of Man, was John the Baptist, Elijah, Jeremiah, or many other great men of faith and power from the past, raised from the dead. Their answer to this question was to link Jesus as the Son of Man to great men of God from the past. What was occurring in these responses was a manifestation of the deception that blinded the eyes of their heart from seeing the divinity of Jesus as the Son of Man. Paul clearly articulates this deception in 2 Cor. 4:4 when he states, "the god of this world has blinded the minds of the unbelievers, to keep them from seeing the light of the gospel of the glory of Christ, who is the image of God." Ultimately the crowds are attempting to appropriate what they have seen in the last years of Jesus' ministry by linking it to some of the powerful men of the past who have moved in the supernatural before.

Jesus was asking this direct question to prod the hearts of his disciples to respond from revelation rather than rehearsed information. Jesus doesn't build his Church on information, he builds his Church on a people who receive heavenly revelation that transforms the trajectory of their life to deny themselves and follow him. If the relationship one holds with Christ is dependent on another person's information and is void of personal revelation, the response one gives when Jesus asks, "Who do you say I am?" will be mere rhetoric that holds no power to actually enable one to follow him.

"But what about you?" he asked. "Who do you say I am?"
Matt. 16:15

Jesus continues digging to the depths of their hearts, moving past "What do others say?" to "What do you say?" He locks in by asking this question because he needs them to know who he is before he unloads on them what is going to come next in his life. Again, the connotation of the Son of Man referred to in Daniel 7:13-14 was one who was going to conquer by being given glory, honor, and praise across the planet. Jesus would go on to tell his disciples that he would be despised to the point of death. By continuing to prod this question he was hoping to draw out of their hearts personal revelation that they could hold onto when the Son of Man was being executed at the cross. Christ's crucifixion was going to offend every Jewish mind, including the disciples'. Their eyes were veiled from seeing that the prophesied son of man would receive all authority in heaven and earth through the path of death and resurrection.

He also wanted to make it clear that the primary purpose of declaring himself as the Son of Man wasn't to prove what he could do but to state who he is. Jesus wanted his disciples to receive the revelation that knowing who he is, is knowing what he can do, not vice versa. Jesus said that signs and wonders would accompany false prophets who were to come (Matt. 24:24). If their revelation of his identity as the Son of Man rested on his supernatural manifestation of power, they would quickly be deceived into believing that others—who actually are not—are the coming Son of Man.

Jesus was about to go on and state that he will build the Church. This statement is stunning, and Jesus is wanting his disciples to know that he has been given authority to build the new covenant people that has been prophesied to Israel for thousands of years. With all that is stated above, Jesus primarily prodded this question personally because he needed them to be rooted in the right answer. Being rooted in the right answer is a critical revelation if we are going to recognize who he is and fully follow him.

Their response of declaring others' revelation and information in verse 14 continues to this day. Jesus continually speaks to our heart for the purpose of drawing us nearer in relationship with him. When we rely on the information or revelation from others and are void of our own, we set ourselves up to be swayed by the waves of information or revelation that run rampant about the Son of Man, rather than being firmly rooted in our own spiritual revelation of Jesus. Jesus' primary point in continuing to prod this question is so that we would know his unique identity as the Son of Man.

Simon Peter answered, "You are the Messiah, the Son of the living God."
Matt. 16:16

Daniel had been given a portion of the revelation as he prophesied in Daniel 7:13 that the one who would be given all authority across the earth was a man. However, the revelation that the one who would be given authority to reign and rule forever was a man was a portion of revelation of the future coming of the King. The revelation that Peter received was remarkable. As stunning as it was to Daniel that a man would be given all authority, he did not know that this Son of man would be the Messiah, the Son of the living God. What Peter declared in this moment about Jesus' identity was a revelatory insight that had never been recognized by humanity before.

Peter receives the most remarkable revelation that had occurred up to this point in human history. His revelation that Jesus is the Messiah, the Son of the living God revealed the depths of who the Son of Man is. This statement is more than a few phrases of theology identifying the identity of Jesus. It is a revelation of the reality that God has come in the flesh through his Son who is going to conquer Satan and sit enthroned as the King of the world forever. Peter is declaring that Jesus is the prophesied anointed one of God. Not only that, but his revelation is declaring that the Son of Man is not of the race of Adam, born from conception of humanity, but the Son of God conceived from heaven.

The simplicity of the answer that Peter gave had profound implications on his life. The wisdom of man that was rooted in religious systems of thought rejected the Son of Man that was given to them as a gift from God. However, God's wisdom was to build the body of Christ through a people who received divine revelation of Jesus' identity. The wisdom of God that is found solely in Christ is foolish to the wisdom of this world (1 Cor. 1:18-19). If we are going to let Christ build his Church, we are going to have to receive him as wisdom from God (1 Cor. 1:24). Like Peter, the revelation that the Son of Man is the Messiah, the Son of the living God, is going to empower us to make disciples and by faith let Christ build his Church.

Jesus replied, "Blessed are you, Simon son of Jonah, for this was not revealed to you by flesh and blood, but by my Father in heaven."
Matt. 16:17

Jesus delights in the revelation that his Father just unleashed on Peter. Out of pure ecstatic joy Jesus addresses Peter by his full name saying "Blessed are you, Simon son of Jonah." Jesus wasn't excited because Peter had theologically understood a reference to the Old Testament, but rather that his heart had just comprehended the reality of life. Because of this, Jesus says you are blessed with the greatest gift ever given humanity which is revelation of my true identity.

This statement Peter made concerning the identity of Jesus didn't come with a mere doctrinal understanding of the Old Testament, connecting it to the reality of what was happening right before him. Though doctrine is necessary and helpful for understanding texts, revelation only occurs as the Father in heaven unveils the eyes of our heart to see the identity of the Son of Man. Jesus was declaring that the only way he can be known, which is through revelation given by his Father in heaven, had happened to Peter in this moment. This revelation has continued to occur the last two thousand years as God continues to reveal the reality of his Son to humanity.

Like Peter, Paul was given this divine revelation that led him to abandon the zealous religiosity he was yoked to. As a "Pharisee of Pharisees" Paul was elite in his intellectual understanding of the text of the Old Testament. However, when receiving revelation that everything he knew was found in Christ, he went off the rails, throwing away "godly" human wisdom and fully relying on Christ to build what his zealous self-dependent effort was attempting to accomplish. His letters testify to this truth as time and time again he declares that what the world so desperately desires will never be found in his wise rhetoric of words but rather in the powerful revelation given by God.

This revelation given by the Father in heaven continues to this day. It is the revelation of the identity of Jesus given by God the Father, which empowers our mission to solely preach, proclaim, and demonstrate Christ crucified and to fully rely on Jesus to build his Church. Without an increasing personal revelation of the power of this truth, we will lack the faith and dependence on Jesus to do what he promised. Consequently, we may end up attempting to build with zealous self-dependent effort what only Jesus' power can build. This revelation isn't a one-time sealing but a continual filling that empowers us to fully rely on Jesus to do what he promised he would.

"And I tell you that you are Peter, and on this rock I will build my church, and the gates of Hades will not overcome it."
Matt. 16:18

It is in this verse that we get to the crux of Jesus' message as he declares that he is going to build the most powerfully divine organism of life through a people he will create to be radical lovers and warriors called the Church. He does this on the foothills of a demonic city staring at a huge rock, declaring that Peter is a piece of the larger rock of revelation. It is on the rock of revelation—that Jesus is God-man in flesh coming as the Messianic Son of Man—that he will build his Church.

As Jesus' disciples are staring at a prophetic symbol of the gates of hades, he declares that he will build his ecclesia, a people group who will carry governing authority. As they stare at what was known as the portal to the demonic underworld Jesus says that the people he will build will overcome the demonic rage of Satan to advance his kingdom across earth. Essentially, Jesus is saying I am going to build the most powerful and purposeful people on planet earth, a people that will prevail victorious over the greatest enemy on the earth. This is a revelatory statement that if not taken hold of as truth can cause the Church that Jesus is building to become one of timid victims rather than victorious warriors. Simply put, the Church that Jesus is building is purposed to reign and rule with him over the demonic principality, powers, and spiritual forces that set themselves up in this age against the intimate knowledge of God being manifested on earth as it is in heaven.

As Peter's name literally means rock, Jesus was declaring that he builds his Church, not merely on a man named Peter, but a body who knows their identity as God's people. Jesus is the builder of the Church and it is critical that we know what he builds with. Our revelation, both individually and collectively, of our royal identity as his people is critical. The living stones he has chosen to build with is us. If we are going to offer ourselves as building blocks to Christ so that he builds his Church, we are going to have to have personal and collective revelation of our identity as his people (1 Pet. 4-5). Knowing who we are is critical in order for him to build that which he desires to build. Though the presence of God could dwell in buildings built by human hands, the material he uses to build the temple of the living God is people. It is in this building formed by his people that his presence and power dwells so that his purposes prevail.

There is critical revelation we need corporately that the Church is not an institutional organization that is created by the "godly" systems of man. The Church is solely the people of God who are being built together by Christ Jesus himself. He is the builder and we are the stones that he has chosen to build with. When we attempt to take authority to become the builder, we will neglect our call to make disciples, attempting to do the job that only Jesus can. Nowhere in Scripture do we find a call to believers to build or plant the Church. The commission that Jesus gave us the authority and command to fulfill is to plant the gospel and make disciples, letting him build his Church. We need a continual revelation that we are the stones Jesus is building with, consequently surrendering and submitting to him to build the Church. Jesus is delivering the Church from the yoke of self-dependence, and building the most powerful presence-based people on planet earth (Eph. 2:19-22).

"I will give you the keys of the kingdom of heaven; whatever you bind on earth will be bound in heaven, and whatever you loose on earth will be loosed in heaven."
Matt. 16:19

What is remarkable is that Jesus is declaring that not only is he going to build his Church by the authority given him from his Father, he is also going to impart to them the authority to reign and rule with him across the earth (Rom. 5:17). What Jesus is doing with what he is building is issuing forth the keys of the kingdom of heaven. He is commissioning forth his disciples into a powerful ministry of manifesting the kingdom of heaven on earth. He is doing this by bestowing on them the access keys to the realm of heaven to authoritatively exercise the realities of that realm here on earth.

These keys that represent authority also depict the reality that there are closed doors that are preventing the manifestation of heaven on earth. Jesus is implying that he is giving them the power to unlock those doors that prevent his power and presence from being made known on planet earth. He commissions them saying, "whatever you bind on earth will be bound in heaven." Jesus similarly taught in Mark that the only way you can plunder the space that a strongman has occupied is by binding him up (Mk. 3:27). The authority that Jesus has given us to "bind on earth" is a commission to see the spaces where Satan sits enthroned as a strongman, tying him to render his presence powerless. As stated in Mark 3:27, once the strongman is bound then we can enter into the space he has occupied and loose the realities of Christ's reign for the purpose of others being propelled into heaven's freedom.

Though you may not know or see the realities of the angelic/demonic heavenly realm, it is more eternally real than that which is seen. The battle at hand is not one against flesh and blood, no matter how demonic a behavior a human being is exhibiting. Our battle lies within an unseen spiritual realm that has a primary mission of shutting the gates from the Kingdom of God invading the earth. When we use our God-given authority to bind and loose to battle against the behavior of man, we become blinded to the real war at hand. Wicked and rebellious behavior manifested from humanity is a byproduct of the demonic stronghold that has taken root in another's life. When we attack and battle against the bad behavior, it is as if we are cutting off the fruit of a bad tree believing that if that bad fruit is taken off of the tree it will become good. While all the while we have been given an authoritative ax to chop down the tree itself and pull out the root that is causing the manifestation of the bad fruit. Satan is the demonic root that we have been given authority to bind on earth so that heaven may be loosed over others' lives.

It is critical that we know that our spiritual authority is primarily empowered by Christ's love for humanity. The governing authority that we carry to reign and rule in life with Christ is for the benefit of others encountering the powerful presence of Jesus. Yes, without love we are nothing. But it is our love that empowers our heart to be burdened and broken for all that hell is currently heaping on humanity. Love empowers our authority to rightfully reign and rule with Jesus, binding the shackles and chains with which Satan is imprisoning many. If your love leads to merely lengthy discussion posts on social media about injustices being done, it is merely a clanging bell. The ecclesia was meant to be an agent of love that carries the authority of Jesus to bind demonic strongholds that Satan is inflicting and that then looses the realities of heaven's healing over humanity. What a privileged people we are to be chosen and commissioned by the King of the world to execute his heart's desire across the earth.

Sam's Personal Journey

On a personal note, the theme of this chapter worked out historically in my life experience. In my twenties, the beginning of the ministry, I was full of vim and vigor, giving myself fully to growing and planting churches. I even turned down multiple offers from denominations to join their organizations to do the same. I wanted to build and plant churches that were most like the Book of Acts that anyone had seen. I wanted them to be biblical, Spirit-led, missional, and unencumbered by traditional bureaucracy. And if you would have asked me then, I was hitting the bullseye.

Then it happened. In the middle of another church plant I clearly sensed the Lord say to me, "You are planting Ishmael and I want Isaac." It shocked me. It made me pause. And though I was about thirty-two at the time and still full of youthful pride, the Spirit had tenderized my heart enough to respond to clear loving rebukes from Him. I knew from my Bible that this word from the Lord to me was bad news. And that it clearly meant that, like Abraham, I was trying to produce something in my own effort that only He was to produce. Further then, the Spirit drew me to Matthew 16 pointing out how Jesus said, "I will build my Church." "I." It was like it was being screamed into the inner chambers of my heart. Then, being a Bible-guy, I began to search the rest of the New Testament to see if I could find any verse that told men to build or plant the church. Much to my consternation I could not. So as an act of integrity, and with my wife's full agreement, we disassembled the "church plant" and started some business so we could still keep eating food, and began to meet in houses with saints.

Through the process I became very anti-institutional. I was passionate about Jesus being the only builder of the Church. And that the Church He was building was a people, not a building or an organization, views which I still passionately hold today. I even began to find many believers as well as leaders who were going through the same process. It was a rich, liberating time.

But I have a natural tendency to go whole hog on things that are very important to me. Where I had spent my first ten years of ministry trying to get people into the "church," I now spent a lot of time trying to get people out of the "church." At some point in that process the Lord spoke to me again saying, "You are doing it again. I didn't tell you to get people into or out of the "institutional church." I told you to make disciples and equip the saints. So we began an equipping ministry about twenty years ago that has multiplied into various forms and fashions.

I am so thankful for the journey we went through that has not only taught us the word but caused our lives to become a word about the reality that Jesus builds the Church and we make disciples. Knowing the difference determines whether you might be mistakenly, even if sincerely, trying to build something that only Jesus can build or whether you are part of something that the gates of hades cannot prevail against.

The Bridegroom Betrothing His Bride

For as a young man marries a young woman, so your sons will marry you; and as a bridegroom rejoices over his bride, so your God will rejoice over you.

Isa. 62:5

There are many relational realities that we partake of in Christ. From sons and daughters to friends and companions the relational paradigm we have with Christ is nuanced in nature. One of these relational paradigms we have in Christ is bride to bridegroom. Jesus is building his Church not only as an agent of power, but also as a beautiful bride adorned as the reward of his suffering. This love saga between Christ and the Church was prophesied from the beginning of creation. Let that sink into your soul for a moment. Before the foundations of the earth were fashioned and formed, God predestined that the sons of men created from the dust of the earth would be the bridal prize for his most precious Son, who would become a bridegroom king.

Adam spoke for all of humanity but was also prophetically speaking of the coming of the Son of God when he declared, "a man shall leave his father and mother and be united with his wife, and the two shall become one flesh" (Gen. 2:24). He was declaring the coming of Christ and the unification in marriage that he would

74

have with his Church (Eph. 5:32). Again, In Genesis 24 we see Abraham sending out a servant to find a wife for his promised son Isaac (Gen. 24:1-4). This was a foreshadow of the Holy Spirit who would be sent out as a servant on behalf of the Son of God to find a bride of beauty. From Adam, Abraham, and beyond, Christ's coming as a bridegroom to be united with his bride has been prophetically uttered from the foundations of the world.

A Glorified Bridegroom and Bride

"To the one who conquers, I will grant to sit with me on my throne as I have conquered and sat with my Father on his throne."
Rev. 3:21

When we approach Jesus for the purpose of giving him everything without receiving anything, he consequently gives us everything his Father gave him (Rom. 8:32). What a glorious promise is given to those who conquer, that he will share the seat of his throne to glorify you in the presence of his Father, rewarding you forever to reign and rule with him. If this statement doesn't ignite in you a fire of gratitude and love for God because of his goodness, I am not sure what would. This promise Jesus spoke in Revelation 3:21 is one of many gifts that he desires to give as he glorifies his bride at his return. We are going to have an eternal intimate love relationship with Christ for billions of years as we reign and rule with him in beauty and righteousness forever.

At his return, Jesus is going to be glorified and worshipped across the world (Mal. 1:11). It is going to be his supremacy that fills the earth, healing us all from the presence and power that Satan has had in this age. Jesus is going to be led in with the Ancient of Days, taking his throne in the world to judge and redeem. It is at this throne that we each will be judged by fire and rewarded according to what we have done during our life on earth (Matt. 16:27, 1 Cor. 3:13-15 , Rev. 22:12). Jesus deeply desires on that day as he releases his fire that a plethora of precious stones will be what has been stored throughout your life so that he can betroth you to himself, rewarding and glorifying you individually and the Church collectively.

This reality is one that needs to be increasingly revealed to our hearts so that we continue to throw off the lesser lovers that we allow to consume the affections of our lives. The Church was destined for eternal beauty to reign and rule forever. If we are going to fully inherit the glorification that Jesus desires to betroth us to, we have to continually choose to deny and die to ourselves and offer him our heart. It is in this posture that we will present ourselves to him at his return with what he is worthy and due to receive. Bridegroom Jesus will have an anointed bride, fully walking in the first commandment, to reign and rule with forever.

The Birth Pains of the Bridegroom and Bride

"For a long time I have held my peace; I have kept still and restrained myself; now I will cry out like a woman in labor; I will gasp and pant."
Isa. 42:14

If we knew the passionate desire our bridegroom king has to receive us, the posture in which we do Church life would radically change. Though Jesus is seated in glory he continues to long for his most desired prize, his bride. The promise that Jesus' Father gave him in Psalm 2:8 to ask and receive his inheritance has yet to be obtained by him. Jesus could have obtained leadership as king over planet earth at his first coming when Satan offered him the kingdoms of the world and as people persistently attempted to make him king by force. However, reigning and ruling over slaves was never his desire. His greatest desire was and is to reign and rule with sons and daughters who collectively offer themselves as his bride. This longing in Jesus' heart has yet to be fulfilled and thus he continues to passionately persist in intercession asking for those entangled in slavery to become sons and for broken lives to be restored into a beautified bride (Rom. 8:34). As described in Isaiah 42:14, he continues to intercede in hope asking with intense pain for his greatest desire to come to fruition.

Though the Father could release his Son to return to planet earth at any moment he is waiting for a bride that longs for her husband as much as her husband longs for her. In God's power he could release his Son to be united with his bride at any time, but in his wisdom he is waiting. He does this because he isn't in the business of creating arranged marriages for his Son but rather longs to offer him a burning, passionate, freely yielded, loving bride.

Jesus is waiting for a bride who passionately will desire the day of their wedding as much as he does. The same intense pain that Jesus is carrying in his heart for the birth of his bride to be one with him is meant to be in our hearts as well. The pain of childbirth is a prophetic image of the intense desire that Jesus has for us. He is waiting for us to have this desire for him (Rom. 8:22-23). Revelation 22:17 sums up the culmination of the bride's last cry before Christ's coming. Though Jesus could have described the passionate cry before his return as a zealous army, a passionate son, or a devoted friend, he chose to describe the cry of the church as a bride. He did this because armies, sons, and friends will never carry the intense desire for intimate union that a bride will. Before the return of Jesus, the bride of Christ will join with the cry of the Spirit of God passionately saying "maranatha," meaning "come Lord Jesus!" Generations have known Jesus as God, Son of God, king, friend, and brother. However the primary relationship with Jesus of the last generation in human history is going to be birthed in the paradigm of a bride to groom. It is going to be this generation that has the hungriest, deepest, and most desperate desire for the marriage of the lamb and the return of her bridegroom king! It is going to be the Church that endures the rage of Satan, bringing an end to this age and transitioning us to the next. Ultimately, the supremacy of Jesus filling the entirety of the world is dependent on a bride, the Church, that burns as a passionate lover partnering with her eternal husband to usher in his reign across the earth (Mt. 24:14).

The Preparation of the Bride

"Let us rejoice and exult and give him the glory, for the marriage of the Lamb has come, and his Bride has made herself ready; it was granted her to clothe herself with fine linen, bright and pure - for the fine linen is the righteous deeds of the saints."
Rev. 19:7-9

If Father God allowed his Son to suffer at the hands of the unrighteous for the purpose of exalting him to the highest place entrusting him all authority, what makes us think he wouldn't refine us in a similar way? Though Jesus suffered agonizing pain for a season, this suffering was purposed so that he could inherit the promise and be propelled to reign and rule in power forever. Though Satan attempts to steal away the gift of suffering, creating an interpretation that suffering is a means of punishment or retribution, there is a deeper purpose that if revealed will create in you joy in the midst of temporary pain, knowing that seasons of suffering come with promises of God's glorious rewards.

Suffering is the refining process that sanctifies us into a bridal prize that our bridegroom king is worthy to receive. Though our flesh hates the momentary pain of suffering, if embraced with faith and hope, on the other end of enduring seasons of suffering is a sanctification that transforms you into a greater glory of Christ's likeness (1 Peter 4:1-2, 5:10). It is in suffering that our weakness thrusts us into the throne room of heaven and the love chambers of Jesus' heart to offer ourselves afresh as a vulnerable, weak, and willing bride in need of a lover's tender touch of intimacy and strength. Suffering isn't meant for your personal pain because of a wrathful rebuke, it is meant to lead you to what your soul aches to satisfy—intimacy with your bridegroom king.

The righteous deeds the saints are clothed in (Rev. 19:9) are ultimately the acts of obedience to God. None of us can learn to live a lifestyle of obedience in a way that Jesus didn't. In Hebrews 5:8 we see that "Jesus learned obedience through what he suffered." What a remarkable statement that often is neglected and rarely embraced by the bride of Christ. If radical obedience to God in this earthly life is the determining factor of being eternally clothed in garments of glory, and suffering is the process by which we learn increasing levels of obedience, then our embrace of suffering will become one of joyful endurance.

Though there is a glorious reward in knowing that we are going to be eternally clothed in glory because we embrace the act of preparing ourselves as Christ's bride, ultimately the purpose of our preparation is to offer Jesus what he deserves. Without a revelation that Jesus was slaughtered as a loving husband we will never present ourselves to him as a fully yielded and surrendered bride. We faithfully embrace this process of preparation, in order for Christ to receive his inheritance. Our suffering serves the supremacy of Christ, as our preparation hastens his return to earth. We are preparing ourselves as a beautiful bride to give to him the reward of his suffering and consequently receive the intimate reward of an eternal marriage.

"For I feel a divine jealousy for you, since I betrothed you to one husband, to present you as a pure virgin to Christ. But I am afraid that as the serpent deceived Eve by his cunning, your thoughts will be led astray from a sincere and pure devotion to Christ."
1 Cor. 11:2-3

Paul's writings give us incredible insight into the bridal paradigm that is written throughout the Bible. Paul's primary concern in ministry was that Jesus receive his inheritance. Thus, Paul deliberately confronted everything that stood in the way of Jesus receiving the affections of the Church, desiring the Church be set free from a love that had grown lukewarm. In 1 Corinthians 11:2 he says, "I am jealous for you with a godly jealousy. For I promised you to one husband, to present you as a pure virgin to Christ." The jealousy that consumed Paul's mission was that Jesus would receive what was due him. Anything that stood in the way of that, Paul realized, was demonically inspired in attempts to steal away Jesus' treasured reward in his bride. He continues saying, "I am afraid, however, that just as Eve was deceived by the serpent's cunning, your minds may be led astray from your simple and pure devotion to Christ" (1 Cor. 11:3). The simplicity of what satisfies Christ is his bride's pure passionate devotion to him.

As were Eve and the church of Corinth, we too can easily become deceived, allowing our minds to be led astray to lesser lovers that have a form of godliness but lack intimate devotion to Christ. The Holy Spirit confronts us for the purpose of preparing us. It is the conviction of the Holy Spirit that confronts where we have become complacent, comfortable, and in control that leads us back to our first love, purely and passionately devoting ourselves to Christ alone.

Jesse's Personal Journey

Personally, the relational paradigm with Jesus as a bridegroom king has shifted the posture of my heart and the trajectory of my mission in life. Though I always had an intellectual understanding that Jesus loved me, it wasn't until I received personal revelation that not only did he love me but that he wanted to marry me did the understanding of my relational journey with him change.

A few years ago, the zealous passion for the manifestation of the Kingdom of God across my city began to rise in my heart. I began to fast and pray with an urgent fervency that never had occurred in my life before. While the posture of my heart was for the purposes of God to prevail, one day while fasting and praying I heard Jesus whisper to my heart saying, "Warriors take the land, and lovers enjoy the plenty. You have taken the land as a warrior, but neglected my greatest desire as a lover. Come as my lover, Jesus said, and enjoy the plenty in the pasture of my presence."

This word radically altered the trajectory of my life, as I laid down my zealous effort to build for him his Kingdom. This word thrust me into a new season of seeking solely after him. It was in this pursuit for a passionate love relationship with him that the beauty and glory of who he was began to mesmerize my life. While the hunger and thirst to build for him his Kingdom was pure, much of it was rooted in my own zealous effort. It was in this season that I began to increase with a hunger and thirst to encounter intimacy in his presence in a way I never had before. I began to realize that warriors make terrible lovers but lovers make unbelievable warriors. It wasn't that my desire for the manifestation of his Kingdom decreased but rather that a revelatory lifestyle of beholding his beauty as his bride increased. It was within this season that yokes and expectations to accomplish for him were broken, and I was set free to fully and confidently rely on him to do what he promised he would.

It has been in this relational revelation the past years that my heart has begun to burn, not to be on a public platform of ministry but to be in the secret love chambers of his heart. I realized as I gazed at his beauty hour after hour that his most desired gift wasn't my zealous missional effort but the affections of my heart. I can't begin to describe in words the freedom from religious performance and the fear of man that occurred as a result of living a lifestyle of being his bride and beholding his beauty.

Though I have many dreams and desires to partner with Jesus as a warrior, Jesus continues to pull me close to his heart as a lover and whisper, "Let your greatest dream be to increasingly intimately know me." Radical lovers truly do make the most devoted warriors.

CHAPTER SIX

Jesus: One Who Baptizes with the Spirit - His Dwelling and Indwelling

The Supremacy of Jesus finds its highest manifestation in the presence of the Holy Spirit. This is a loaded statement that we each need personal revelation of if we are going to partner with Jesus' mission that he be supreme in all things. Throughout this chapter we will break down how Jesus' supremacy is manifested through a people who partner with the power and presence of the Holy Spirit.

The Prophesied Promise

The supremacy of Jesus being manifested through the presence of the Holy Spirit was prophesied throughout all of the Old Testament. The law that was given to Moses and commanded to be kept by the people was a gift that revealed the need for a savior. This law that many lived under before Christ wasn't the promise, rather it revealed the need for a greater law that would be given by the power and presence of the Holy Spirit (Rom. 7:9-11). While the law in and of itself wasn't evil (Rom. 7:7), it revealed the sinful nature of the human heart and the inability of our hearts to walk in obedience to God. The prophesied promise was the coming of a savior who would take away the sins of the world and baptize the human heart with the Holy Spirit (Gal. 4:6). While a coming Messiah was prophesied a plethora of times so was a new era in which the Holy Spirit would not just visit but make humanity His dwelling place. This Holy Spirit was prophesied to bring about a life-giving new nature, restoring humanity back to God's original intent for us to have continual relationship with him.

"For this is the covenant that I will make with the house of Israel after those days, declares the Lord: I will put my law within them, and I will write it on their hearts. And I will be their God, and they shall be my people."
Jer. 31:33

The law that was written on tablets of stone to be kept by people was prophesied to be written on the tablets of hearts. While the written law articulated God's heart for his people's obedience and freedom, it was merely words written on stone. However, Jeremiah prophesied that the law that was written by the pen of man would be written by the ink of the Holy Spirit on the human heart. The law of the Spirit isn't a new set of ten commandments, but rather a glorious impartation of the Holy Spirit from heaven into our heart that transforms us to desire God. This law is a powerful inward presence that now dwells within us. Not only would God dwell among us, but Jeremiah is prophesying that he will dwell IN us. This indwelling of the law of the Spirit empowers us to walk in obedience to God and live in the freedom he intended for us, not by our own strength and effort but by his.

"And afterward, I will pour out My Spirit on all people. Your sons and daughters will prophesy, your old men will dream dreams, your young men will see visions. Even on My menservants and maidservants, I will pour out My Spirit in those days."
Joel 2:28-29

The "afterward" that Joel was referring to when he prophesied this outpouring was the crucifixion, resurrection, and ascension of Jesus Christ. What was limited to God's chosen people and the nation of Israel, Joel prophetically proclaimed would be given to all of the nations as the outpouring of the Holy Spirit would know no bounds. It was through this prophesied outpouring that a people would receive the indwelling of the Holy Spirit.

This promise that was prophesied was critical, as it was the passage that Peter declared had occurred immediately preceding Pentecost (Acts 2:17-18). Though Peter could have made many proclamations in that moment, being inspired by the Holy Spirit to reference this passage is important. Joel prophesied and Peter affirmed that when the Spirit of God was poured out it would result in a people who prophesied. We now know that the spirit of prophecy bears testimony to Jesus (Rev. 19:10) and is primarily purposed for the increase of Jesus' supremacy. Through the indwelling of the Holy Spirit all sons and daughters of God partner in making Christ supreme in all things by prophesying. Simply put, the Holy Spirit being poured on our lives empowers us to speak Spirit-inspired words. It is this spirit of prophecy that supernaturally manifests the existence and supremacy of the Son of God.

"I will give you a new heart and put a new spirit within you; I will remove your heart of stone and give you a heart of flesh. And I will put

My Spirit within you and cause you to walk in My statutes and to
carefully observe My ordinances."
 - Ez. 36:26-27

The power to participate in righteousness and holiness was never meant to be attained by the strength of our own effort. Ezekiel prophesied that God would impart his Spirit into the human heart that became soft like flesh and consequently, would empower them to obey and follow him by his presence rather than their effort. What was being prophesied was the outpouring of the law of the Spirit that would give life, setting humanity free from the law of sin and death (Rom. 8:2).

Before the coming of Christ and the outpouring of the Holy Spirit, the affections of the human heart were hard toward God. The nature of our flesh disempowered us from walking in communion with God and in step with the nature of who he is. God's promise to remove a heart of stone and give us a heart of flesh is what readies us to receive his Spirit to commune with him in obedience and joy.

The next day he saw Jesus coming toward him, and said, "Behold, the
Lamb of God, who takes away the sin of the world! I myself did not
know him, but he who sent me to baptize with water said to me, 'He on
whom you see the Spirit descend and remain, this is he who baptizes
with the Holy Spirit.' And I have seen and have borne witness that this
is the Son of God."
 John 1:29, 33-34

John the Baptist, the forerunner who paved the way for Jesus' first coming, prophetically declares the mission and purpose of the life of Jesus. John the Baptist proclaimed in John 1 two primary things about Jesus, 1) "Behold, the Lamb of God, who takes away the sin of the world!" (John 1:29) and 2) "He on whom you see the Spirit descend and remain, this is he who baptizes with the Holy Spirit" (John 1:33). The language John uses to declare Jesus as the lamb of God is significant as it would have been language related to the passover that gave context of sacrifice for sins. John the Baptist was prophetically declaring that there was going to be a redemptive and restorative work done on humanity through the sacrificial lamb of God, Jesus Christ, who would take away the sins of the world, baptizing humanity with the Holy Spirit.

The first, the lamb of God slain for the sins of the world, is the means to the second, the baptism of the Holy Spirit. Our redemption by the blood of Jesus makes the way for the baptism of the Holy Spirit. The baptism of the Holy Spirit occurs through the union with the man, Christ Jesus (1 Cor. 6:17, Rom. 6:3, Gal. 3:27). This union only occurs because of the crucifixion, resurrection, and ascension of Christ.

Remarkably, the Church assumes a mantle like that of John the Baptist's mantle, forerunning Jesus' second coming by the power of the prophetic proclamation that John the Baptist made about Jesus in his first coming. Jesus makes a stunning statement in Matthew 11:11 saying, "Truly, I say to you, among those born of women there has arisen no one greater than John the Baptist. Yet the one who is least in the kingdom of heaven is greater than he." The transformational power that John the Baptist prophesied would be poured out he did not partake in. Let that sink into your soul a moment. This power of the presence of the Holy Spirit that John the Baptist prophesied would occur through the life of Jesus transforms you into a creation that is greater than the greatest man ever born of a woman before Christ. It is through the life of Christ and the indwelling of the Holy Spirit that the supremacy of Christ is manifested first in our lives and then through our lives.

"It is to your advantage that I go away, for if I do not go away, the Helper will not come to you. But if I go, I will send him to you."
John 16:7

It is hard two thousand years later to grasp the gravity and weight of the statement that Jesus is making to his disciples above. The companion that the disciples had when Jesus made this statement was him. Their context and commitment for following God was Jesus. His statement that it was better for him to leave would have been perplexing and potentially quite disturbing to the hearts of his disciples.

This statement holds critical significance to the purposes of God and the plans to enhance his Son's supremacy and manifest it throughout the world. While Jesus could have reigned across the regions of Israel during his first coming, his plan to inhabit the whole earth with his glory went far beyond participation with him in the flesh. Jesus' statement references our purpose amidst his plan today. The death, resurrection, and ascension of Jesus paved the way for the outpouring of the Holy Spirit and the first fruit fulfillment of his prayer in John 17:21-24.

"Exalted to the right hand of God, Jesus has received from the Father the promised Holy Spirit and has poured out what you now see and hear ... the promise is for you and your children and for all who are far off—for all whom the Lord our God will call."
Acts 2:33, 39

Though the timeline of Jesus' life that Peter is preaching may seem simple, the explanation and revelation of what Jesus had fulfilled was astounding. Peter is explaining that the death, resurrection, ascension, and outpouring of the Holy Spirit had all been prophesied throughout all of the Old Testament. He is explaining that this revelation is being manifested through their lives on the day of Pentecost. His explanation for their behavior is rooted in the reality that Jesus is the Son of God who has conquered death and now poured out the prophesied promise over their lives by filling them with the Holy Spirit (Acts. 2:23-29).

Jesus ascended into heaven and received the promised Holy Spirit so that he could pour out the Holy Spirit in a way the Spirit had never been poured out before. This pouring out had been prophesied many times leading up to Jesus' life. This prophesied promise of the outpouring of the Holy Spirit redemptively created in humanity a restoration of what Satan had stolen, restoring humanity into a new nature never seen before Christ (2 Cor. 5:17). This outpouring also transformed humanity into a walking temple in which God's presence dwelt so that collectively, the Church would manifest the supremacy of Christ throughout the entire world.

This glorious plan to inhabit the whole earth was purposed for the partnership the Church would hold through the indwelling of the Holy Spirit. Jesus' supremacy being manifested on earth as it is in heaven comes as a result of a people who dwell in the presence of Jesus and consequently carry his presence that is dwelling in and among them. The increased reality of Jesus' supremacy comes through the surrendered hearts of those who receive and manifest the supernatural presence of the Holy Spirit.

Conversion to Completion

Jesus' primary goal isn't your conversion, sealing you for your seat in heaven. Though this is the beginning of the process, his primary goal is completion, getting heaven into your heart and continually filling you with the Holy Spirit so that you are transformed into the image of the Son (Rm. 8:29). Understanding that the sealing of the Holy Spirit converts you but the filling of the Holy Spirit transforms you is critical to allowing God to bring you into his completed intention.

It is through faith in the life of Christ given by his crucifixion, resurrection, and ascension that we are sealed and then filled with the Holy Spirit. The sealing of the Holy Spirit is a miraculous gift that ensures the salvation of our soul for eternity (Eph. 1:13). However, what a wretched life we live if our hope for all that hell has heaped on humanity is merely rooted in eternity and never experienced presently. The filling of the Holy Spirit isn't merely an intellectual theological understanding but a spiritual reality that literally transforms our souls into the likeness and nature of God (Eph. 4:23-24, Col. 3:10, 1 Jn. 4:17). This continual filling takes us from one level of God's glory to the next (2 Cor. 3:18) fashioning and forming our souls into the righteousness, holiness, and purity of God on earth as it will forever be in heaven (1 Cor. 1:30). The filling of the Holy Spirit is the process of sanctification. The Holy Spirit's sanctifying work results in a growth of the Spirit's Lordship and presence within us.

What a miraculous work the Holy Spirit is doing in the souls of humanity through the body and blood of Jesus. His blood shed and his body broken and then resurrected are an eternal reality of life that fills our souls in the present time as we choose to continually die to self, offering ourselves freely to him (2 Cor. 4:10-11). The pinnacle of life that our souls ache to be satisfied in will not occur on this side of eternity. Though there will be a day where we will see him as he is, immediately becoming like him (1 Jn. 3:2) today is not that day. Though it may sound despairing, this reality actually places us in a position of continual hope, constantly being offered the opportunity to long for and take hold of more of Christ.

90

None of us will ever reach that pinnacle here on earth of the filling of the Holy Spirit. This is a glorious reality that is meant to cause our souls to continually die to self, seeking after Jesus, allowing the Holy Spirit to transform us to be like him. There is a higher and broader place of completion that the Holy Spirit is continually probing our hearts to surrender to. If we choose to embrace this invitation of completion we will intellectually, experientially, and affectionately be transformed by the presence of the Holy Spirit that fills our mind, will, and emotions.

"Therefore do not be foolish, but understand what the will of the Lord is. And do not get drunk with wine, for that is debauchery, but be filled with the Spirit."
Eph. 5:17-18

Each of our souls is being satisfied through the infilling of something. Paul's exhortation to the Church of Ephesus is shining light on this truth. Whether the wine that you drink resides in a glass or in the false pleasures and promises of the world, if it is imbibed instead of Christ you will become like that which you drink. Paul is revealing that our souls are longing to be satisfied and thus being filled with something. This filling is continually happening as we are either drinking the wine of the world or the wine of Christ, the Holy Spirit. The sealing of the Spirit ensures eternal deliverance, but it is the filling of the Holy Spirit that pulls that eternal reality into present time, delivering us now from the devil's grasp and transforming us now into who we will be into eternity.

Waiting on His Presence

Jesus commissioned the disciples to live on an apostolic mission when he sent them to go make disciples of all nations (Matt. 28:19-20). Though they could have immediately begun teaching others to obey what Jesus had instructed them, they had to wait. Making disciples couldn't be done by a mere rhetoric of words Jesus spoke. The disciples needed the powerful indwelling presence of the Holy Spirit that empowered the ministry of Jesus. Following his commission to them to go, he instructed them to wait. Jesus was going to ascend into heaven in resurrected bodily form first and then his Father would pour out through Him the promised Holy Spirit.

The disciples had a high priority for the Holy Spirit. They saw Jesus minister in the power and presence of the Holy Spirit. They understood that if they were going to do even greater things than him, they would need the presence and power of the Spirit that Jesus ministered with (Jn. 14:12). For the disciples, the Spirit of God was the power of their mission, enabling them to literally love God with all their hearts, souls, and minds. Then, they were sent out in the presence and power of the Holy Spirit so that they could execute the Father's will. They knew without the prophesied promise of the Holy Spirit they would be lukewarm lovers, lacking the power to accomplish what Jesus commissioned them to do.

Revelation of the power given through the Holy Spirit is critical if we are going to be empowered by the presence of the Holy Spirit to fulfill the commission that was extended from the first century disciples to us. Often we attempt to make disciples by a series of books, systems, and Sunday mornings. Though none of these are bad, if not empowered by the Holy Spirit, we will attempt to live a life of faithful ministry that has a form of godliness but holds no power. It is the powerful presence of the Holy Spirit that supernaturally empowers us to partner with the mission of Jesus to

92

manifest the reality of his heavenly reign making him supreme on earth as he?? is in heaven. Apart from the presence and power of the Holy Spirit we will live a religious Christian life that promotes and preaches behaviors and forms of Christianity but is void of the testimonial power and presence of the Holy Spirit.

Before heaven invaded earth, earth invaded heaven at the hands of the disciples who fervently prayed asking for the prophesied promise to be poured out on them—the Holy Spirit. If we are honest, we have a difficult time waiting while always wanting to be sent out. Though we can quickly create systems and solutions to attempt to partner with God to fulfill Christ's mission, if we fail to wait and passionately pursue God through prayer, we may live a ministry life that is void of his systems and solutions birthed in and through the Spirit's power and presence. Unfortunately, when void of a life that passionately waits for his presence, the supremacy of man begins to take root and what we claim in the name of God is purposed for our own exaltation. Without the empowerment of the Holy Spirit's presence the primary mission of enhancing Jesus' leadership and supremacy will become secondary to the fame of our own name. The Holy Spirit's primary mission is to exalt Christ in and through our lives. If we are not in constant communion with him, that mission will be non-existent in us and we will create other missions in the name of Jesus that are primarily about us.

Staying in Step

The issue of the fruit we produce from our lives lies within the root we live under, as that which we source from will become the fruit that we produce in our life. Paul is doing more than giving a good teaching, he is highlighting the issue of the human heart and what it is sourcing from to satisfy its longings. Like Adam and Eve, we too can easily source from the tree of the knowledge of good and evil, attempting to obtain things that we consider good that produce just as much death as evil things. Ultimately whether good or bad, if we source from the flesh we will produce death.

While many well-intentioned believers have many methods they create in an attempt to become more holy, it is only in staying in step with the Spirit that we can produce His fruit. The task of seeing the fruit of the flesh thwarted lies within staying in step with the Spirit. The Spirit produces life, while the flesh produces death (Rom. 8:6). The flesh and spirit are the two roots that produce the fruit that manifests from a person's life. If rooted in the flesh the acts of our lives will produce death. If rooted in the Spirit the fruit which we yield will be life.

Through the Holy Spirit the list of the fruits is dynamically produced. Meaning, we don't manufacture or muster up love, peace, patience, etc. Rather these fruits are coming out from the Holy Spirit within us as we participate in faith with him. It takes faith to believe that he exists, lives in us, and that his abiding presence is transforming us into new creations. It is by faith that we participate in the transforming power of the Holy Spirit. We do this by continually dying to ourselves while trusting in the Spirit's life to manifest through us these fruits. Paul's teaching in the following passage reveals these truths and helps articulate how we can learn to live a lifestyle of walking in step with the Holy Spirit.

"So I say, walk by the Spirit, and you will not gratify the desires of the flesh. For the flesh desires what is contrary to the Spirit, and the Spirit what is contrary to the flesh. They are in conflict with each other, so that you are not to do whatever you want."
Gal. 5:16-17

The simplicity of walking in step with the Spirit lies in discerning the difference between our flesh and spirit. Paul's revelation of this reality helps give us context in how to discern what it means to walk in the Spirit. The acts of our flesh primarily are purposed for instantly satisfying ourselves. Paul expounds on these acts saying, "the acts of the flesh are obvious, sexual immorality, impurity and debauchery; idolatry and witchcraft; hatred, discord, jealousy, fits of rage, selfish ambition, dissensions, factions and envy; drunkenness, orgies, and the like" (Gal. 5:19-20). However in direct conflict with the acts of the flesh are the fruit of the Spirit which Paul states is "love, joy, peace, forbearance, kindness, goodness, faithfulness, gentleness and self-control" (Gal. 5:22-23)."

The direct conflict that the flesh and spirit are in is a gift given by God that allows us to discern the devil's tactics and our desires to resist denying ourselves and following Christ. It is the Spirit of God that enlightens us to discern the difference between the flesh and Spirit. Without Christ, by nature we will gratify the desires of the flesh. However, with Christ, the difference between the two becomes obvious. In Christ we are empowered to produce the fruits of the Spirit by his power rather than ours.

"But if you are led by the Spirit, you are not under the law ... Against such things there is no law."
Gal. 5:18, 23

"Those who belong to Christ Jesus have crucified the flesh with its passions and desires."
Gal. 5:24

Christ died for our eternal salvation but he also died so that we may inherit presently the manifestation of his presence. Simply put, he died both for you and as you. This is a remarkable reality that we can only participate in by faith. Christ's crucifixion was meant to become our crucifixion, disempowering the arousing desires and passions of our flesh that lead to death, propelling us into a passionate desire for his powerful presence that leads to life.

Walking in step with the Spirit happens exclusively through the accomplished work of Christ Jesus on the cross. Embracing a life of relying on the presence and power of the Holy Spirit comes not merely through feeling but faith. When we know the victory of the cross of Christ we enter into an active realm of faith, participating by faith in the powerful work of the Holy Spirit within us. It is in this realm of faith that we continue to draw deeper and deeper from the realm of the Spirit. When this occurs our conscious minds, wills, and emotions begin to assimilate to and with the Spirit of God. This is a spiritual work that we partake in by faith, allowing his power to transform us into our new nature (Eph. 3:16). This sanctifying work of the Holy Spirit that produces heaven's fruit from our lives is unending. The more we continually surrender and yield to his active presence, the more we are transformed into carrying and living out the Spirit's fruit.

"Since we live by the Spirit, let us keep in step with the Spirit. Let us not become conceited, provoking and envying each other."
Gal. 5:24-25

Paul's language to exhort us to keep in step with the Spirit is very detailed. Because of this, being dedicated to abiding in the Spirit is the method by which we learn to lean on his presence and power rather than our own. It is in this process that we learn to know the Spirit's presence and promptings that empower us to produce his fruits. This happens through consciously being aware of the Spirit's presence in everyday relationships, tasks, as well as ministry moments.

Practically this looks like learning to hear and respond to the Spirit's checks, promptings, warnings, etc. This is one of my primary goals in discipleship as I am leading others to a life of reliance on the leadership of the Holy Spirit, not me. Paul highlights that conceited envy and jealousy can keep us from personally and collectively keeping in step with the Spirit. The moment that our mission is self-centered is the moment we begin walking in the flesh, consequently rejecting the Spirit. Each of us is personally meant to be empowered by the Spirit of God so that collectively as the Church, we can labor together in unity to manifest his presence, increasing his supremacy across the world.

The Indwelling and Dwelling of The Disciple

The seal of the Holy Spirit on a person's life is the greatest gift ever offered humanity. Understanding the significance of this seal helps us to appreciate and adore the gift we have been given. Throughout the Old Testament there was significance in marks given by kings through the seal of signet rings they wore. The signet ring sealing specific orders made official the execution of particular tasks that the king desired. Much like these signet sealings, through Christ, we are sealed with the Holy Spirit. While these signet seals were significant, they do not compare to the reality of the sealing of the Holy Spirit on a human heart given by King Jesus.

The supernatural seal of the Holy Spirit isn't merely a mark given with authoritative ink that only guarantees our future inheritance in heaven, though that is part of it. This seal is literally the living person of the Holy Spirit, depositing heaven into our hearts in the present time. The seal of the Holy Spirit stamped on our heart is the presence of Christ Jesus himself. This seal empowers us to execute our King's commands with his presence and power. Like the signet ring, the sealing of the Holy Spirit is a decreed declaration from heaven over a human's life to empower them for Christ's mission.

The sealing of the Holy Spirit on the heart of humanity is what the peoples of the nations have desired for all of history. Paul says in Colossians 1:27, "To them God chose to make known how great among the Gentiles are the riches of the glory of this mystery, which is Christ in you, the hope of glory." This mystery was made manifest in the man Christ Jesus and continues to be manifested through Christ indwelling the life of humanity through his promised Holy Spirit. Jesus is both indwelling the disciple and the dwelling place of the disciple by the Holy Spirit. It is our yieldedness to dwell through Christ in the indwelling Holy Spirit that we partake in the life of Jesus.

The reason that we are in Christ is because the Holy Spirit is in us. God's greatest desire has always been union with humanity. Since the fall this restored union could only occur through the indwelling Holy Spirit. Union with Christ is why we were created. Jesus wasn't created for us, we were created through and for him (Jn. 1:3, Col. 1:16). While humans carry many purposes in God's plan, ultimately we are a gift given to Jesus for the reward of his suffering on the cross. Before the foundations and formation of the earth it was predetermined by the eternal counsel of heaven that Jesus, the Son of God, would be sent to earth to restore and redeem that which was lost (Eph. 1:4). The reality of this statement means that the gift of the Holy Spirit is what unifies Christ to be one with us, receiving the reward he most desires. As he becomes one with us through indwelling our hearts with his Spirit, we become one with him by dwelling in what he has indwelled in us. Dwelling in his indwelling empowers us to be in union with him as he is in union with us.

Whether people realize it or not, everyone is searching after the satisfaction found in unity with the trinity. This personal unity is what our souls were fashioned together to be satisfied in. We were fashioned and formed this way so that we would be led to give ourselves to Christ, in order that he receives union with us and us with him. Jesus understood the life found in union, as he constantly declares throughout his ministry that he is in the Father and the Father is in him (Jn. 14:11). It is because of his yieldedness to dwell in the indwelling Holy Spirit that his soul was satisfied with love and joy (Jn. 15:10-11). The same union that Jesus shared in the flesh with his Father is available for us to share with him (Jn. 14:20, 17:21). It is in this unity with him that our souls are satisfied, sharing in the love and joy that is in Christ.

Life manifests itself personally and collectively under the supremacy of Jesus Christ. It is in our union with Christ through the Holy Spirit that his supreme leadership begins to take root in our lives. It is in Christ's supremacy that his presence is most made known and humanity experiences the realities of heaven on earth. In the Old Testament this occurred in a temple that was built by human hands and hosted the presence of God. In this place sat God's supreme authority on earth. The manifestation of his supremacy is his presence and many gathered in this temple to encounter both.

However, God never desired for humanity to build the temple in which he dwelt, he desired for them to be the temple in which he dwelled (Acts 17:24). What was stationary in the Old Testament became mobile in Christ. Like the Old Testament, the heart that has Christ sitting supreme abides in the presence of the Holy Spirit. In this age the highest manifestation of Christ's supremacy occurs through the mobile temple that abides in the presence of God. This mobile temple is both the individual life of the disciple and the collective body of Christ, the Church. The realities that exist in Christ's supreme authority and leadership are manifested from a people who personally and collectively submit to him. We have been given an incredible privilege to partner with the mission of Jesus, through the presence of his Holy Spirit, to make him supreme in all things.

As we continually yield to dwell in the indwelling Holy Spirit, we become like that which is dwelling in us. The divine nature of Christ infiltrating and transforming our lives occurs through the spiritual presence of the Holy Spirit. Partaking in the divine nature of Christ and escaping the destruction and corruption of our sinful nature in the flesh is possible (1 Pet. 1:3-4). Not only is it possible, but it is meant to be the experienced and normal expression of a disciples life who dwells in the indwelling Holy Spirit. Dwelling in him as he is dwelling in you is your deliverance from the nature of your flesh, consequently transforming you into your new divine nature created to be like God in true righteousness and holiness (Eph. 4:24).

It is in this way that Jesus is increasing his supremacy in and through our lives. It is the continued acquisition of the real estate of the affections and the acreage of our heart that Jesus possesses in us that which he rightfully owns. As a mighty warrior, Jesus is most concerned about taking the land of our heart to reign and rule over our lives. It is our agreement to allow him possession of our heart that his supremacy, dominion, and Kingdom increases inwardly and then manifests outwardly from our lives. Today, yield and surrender afresh the affections of your heart, allowing Christ to sit supreme in all things in your life. If you do, the realities of his reign will transform your life into the likeness of Christ, empowering your mission to do that which Jesus is doing.

CHAPTER SEVEN

The Supremacy of Christ, the Central Point of All Spiritual Warfare

Because the supremacy of Christ is the great issue of the universe and time, it is the primary point of spiritual warfare. Knowing the central goal of all warfare can help us focus, endure, and overcome. Though there are a thousand flavors of warfare, the central goal of this spiritual warfare is focused on one thing—to steal and supplant the supremacy of Christ. Satan's primary mission is to take away (steal) that which Christ rightfully deserves in you by replacing (supplementing) in your life other lovers to sit supreme.

I cannot emphasize enough that the central point of Satan's hate is Jesus' supremacy. All the hate he is heaping on humanity is primarily because of his hatred toward Christ receiving what he desires and sitting supreme in all things. Satan is not anti-humanity or even anti-church, he is anti-Christ. Because he hates Christ, he hates us. With passionate zeal he is attacking and attempting to dethrone Christ's reign in and through humanity. This chapter is purposed to help you understand the various dimensions of spiritual warfare, understanding what is happening in your life spiritually. Satan is doing more than just attempting to create frustration, depression, anger, selfishness, and impatience in you.

He is primarily attempting to steal away the affections and focus of your heart and to prevent you from being fixated on the supremacy of Christ.

"For I feel a divine jealousy for you, since I betrothed you to one husband, to present you as a pure virgin to Christ. But I am afraid that as the serpent deceived Eve by his cunning, your thoughts will be led astray from a sincere and pure devotion to Christ."
2 Cor. 11:2-3

Paul had a zealous jealousy for the purity of the bride, realizing one of Satan's primary points of warfare is to attack the Church's purity with Christ. In 2 Cor. 11:3 Paul links the original warfare associated with Eve to the current warfare against every believer. Paul reveals that Satan's goal is to deceive the believers mind for the purpose of distorting devotion to Christ. I believe that this is the core purpose behind every attack from the enemy. Satan doesn't merely want to make us uncomfortable, unhappy, or unsuccessful. The primary mission of Satan is to supplant the preeminence of Christ in our affections and loyalty.

Like Eve, Satan isn't primarily concerned with convincing us to follow him. His primary mission is to create a self-absorbed obsession with ourselves. Even after we are saved, he continues to probe our hearts tempting us to reject denying ourselves, to keep control of our own lives, so as to never give our lives to Christ and thus gain his. In the Garden of Eden Satan provoked the heart of Eve to obtain good knowledge that had a perceived benefit to her. Ultimately, he was distorting the nature of God by creating a false narrative of who he was. By doing so Satan injected into humanity a nature of self exaltation—like his own—that rejected pure faith in the word of God and lured us to become wise in our own eyes.

This simple scheme of Satan has profound implications for our pure devotion to Christ. When the Church becomes wise in her own eyes she formulates and cultivates a Christian walk that has a form of godliness but lacks pure devotion to Jesus alone. At the root of the issue, this is what Paul addresses in his letter to the Church of Corinth. They were continually being swayed back and forth by a variety of "gospels" and "Jesuses" (1 Cor. 11:4). Many were coming in the name of God proclaiming false freedom that could be found in a variety of sources. Paul is shedding light on the reality that when swayed so easily by false messages and narratives that have a form of religious good but aren't Christ himself, there is a gap in the Church's pure devotion to Jesus. This scheme continues to this day as Satan is constantly attempting to sway the Church's heart to lesser lovers that seem religiously good but produce just as much death and destruction as evil things. Jesus alone is the atonement for our sins, the way to life in God, and the hope for eternal salvation. Anything else added to that message is the deception of the devil.

Jesus isn't a point of the gospel, he is the gospel. The deception of the devil is to distort truth by adding false narratives to the gospel of grace. The devil is constantly attempting to steal away our sole devotion to Jesus by probing our minds to create narratives that either take away or add to Christ. While the narratives that are blatantly evil are obvious, many of the narratives Satan attempts to deceive our minds with come as an "angel of light" (2 Cor. 11:14-15). This angel of light message is a manufactured multi-flavored gospel of grace that looks, sounds, and seems good, but if not solely devoted to the supremacy of Jesus it steals away the precious prize Jesus desires from his bride—her undivided, fully devoted, and pure love for him. Within the Church this warfare is one of Satan's primary strategies as he constantly desires for us to lean and rely on good things that steal away our pure and undivided devotion to Jesus.

Narrowing this down, the warfare that works individually in our lives is to deceive our minds. Each of us have strongholds and systems of thought that reside in the affections of our heart and the thought patterns of our mind. What dwells as a habitual system of emotion in our hearts and thought in our minds empowers our will to yield to whatever we believe will produce life. Before Christ, all were alienated from God and enemies in our minds to his life (Col. 1:21). Meaning our wills were bent toward evil because of the natural thought pattern our minds held. By nature we rejected and rebelled against God. However, through the blood and body of Christ our minds have been renewed and reconciled to God, creating in us a new habitual system of thought that by nature yields and submits to God. It is critical that our minds are alert and sober, having revelation that the primary point of our mission is Jesus' supremacy being manifested in all things. If not, we will quickly create and execute mission strategies in the name of God that aren't primarily purposed for Jesus' supremacy. Unfortunately, we can quickly be deceived into having a distorted view, deceived mind, and divided heart toward pure devotion to Christ.

The Strategies of Satan's Schemes

Again, when we consider spiritual warfare we have to evaluate it through the lens of the centrality and supremacy of Christ. In warfare we are not attempting to merely get past unrighteous habits through a process of behavior modification. We are warring for the purpose of getting Christ what he rightfully deserves, which is preeminence in our personal lives. When we see clearly that the strategy of Satan in our personal area of warfare is primarily to suppress and supplant the supremacy of Christ we are empowered to properly battle strongholds by rightfully placing Christ as supreme in all things. When we are rooted in a lifestyle of simplicity and undivided devotion to Christ, freedom begins to be birthed, producing in and through us a rich harvest of righteousness and holiness. As I share common places of warfare, consider how Satan is supplanting Christ's supremacy in your life by replacing it with false pleasures and promises of the world. Simply put, the freedom and life you long for, that Satan is attempting to distort, will be found by placing Christ supreme in all things.

The Preeminence of Pride
God opposes the proud but gives grace to the humble.
James 4:6

The warfare of pride is more than just making us boastful, it is the process that supplants ourselves as preeminent in the place of Jesus. The temptation of pride is to remove a personal and collective culture of humility. The enemy probes at our love of self, stirring up a spirit of pride because humility is the place that is honored by Jesus and that honors Jesus. Immediately preceding the passage above James says, "Or do you suppose it is to no purpose that the Scripture says, "He yearns jealously over the spirit that he has made to dwell in us"? Humility is what empowers our will to surrender to Christ so that we would be imparted with and abide in the spirit that he jealously yearns for. Humility can only flow from hearts that have enthroned Christ as supreme in their affections. Discerning if pride is ruling our soul is incredibly simple and quickly reveals whether Christ is preeminent as the love of our life. Because everything in life we do flows from the affections of our heart, intentionally guarding it from being infected with pride is critical (Prov. 4:23).

God opposes the proud not because of mere bad behavior, but rather because the posture of their hearts are bowed to other gods, giving their affections to others instead of him. The grace that Jesus gives to the humble is a result of the posture of a heart that is pure, passionately abiding in his presence. The word grace in this passage is a greek word, charis. Ultimately grace is getting what you do not deserve. The grace that Jesus gives to the humble is more than a monetary gift. It literally is the presence of the Holy Spirit that has a divine influence that transforms the human heart with a new nature that carries the realities of heaven.

Our submission to Jesus' preeminence postures us in a position to receive God's promises, as humility precedes honor (Prov. 15:33). Spirit empowered humility always catches the eye of heaven, releasing the reward of his life over ours. Satan is seeking to steal away Christ receiving you, and you receiving the rewards that rest in a life that abides in him. The promise that lies in a life of humility is a manifest blessing touching multiple areas of our life (Prov. 22:4, Matt. 23:12). Satan is scheming to steal away from us experiencing the rich reward in the present time of the realities of life in Christ. Pride precedes the destruction the devil desires while humility prepares you to partake in the provision of God's promises (Prov. 16:18). This is one of the primary places of warfare each of us experience day in and day out, as Satan woos our hearts to be puffed in pride rather than surrendered in humility.

The Preeminence of Money

"No one can serve two masters, for either he will hate the one and love the other, or he will be devoted to the one and despise the other. You cannot serve God and money."

Matt. 6:24

In the Sermon on the Mount, Jesus is addressing many issues of warfare that are stealing away the freedom of souls. Jesus is stating that it is impossible to serve both God and money because of the duality of the heart. Meaning, affections of the human heart were created to be solely devoted to one thing, not divided by many things. All of the sins that Jesus highlights as areas of warfare in our lives are about the preeminence of the affections of our heart. The capacity the heart has for radical dedication and devotion is remarkable. The reality Jesus sheds light on is the fact that we all are devoted to a master. The question isn't merely are we devoted to a master, it is "what master are we devoted to?" It is the master we are devoted to that will determine what the affections of our heart hold as our personal precious pearl (Matt. 6:21; 13:44-46).

The lure and seduction of money is centered around supplanting the supremacy of Christ with a false promise of finding the satisfaction of power and purpose in money. The pseudo power found in a life that serves the master of money cultivates a desire to control and take what we want rather than surrender and receive Jesus. The dark master of money promises a life of purpose found in personal exaltation, prosperity, and success in the eyes of the world. This is a counterfeit experience of purpose that comes at a high cost of forfeiting our eternal exaltation, prosperity, and success given in and with Christ. Ultimately the promises of serving money will leave us poorer than before, never satisfying the ache our soul screams to find—our treasure in the person of Jesus Christ.

Money is a seductive substance that attempts to replace reliance on Christ to provide for us. As creatures of God's creation we were created to source life from him to satisfy our souls. When Jesus teaches his disciples to pray he instructs them to ask, "Give us today our daily bread" (Matt. 6:11). This model of prayer was teaching the disciples more than how to receive by faith a lunchtime meal. It was creating in them a lifestyle of sourcing by faith from their Father in heaven. The glorious gift that is given when we source life from God is the experiential reality of the substance of his Son. Jesus is the Word of God that is much more than words written on a page, he is a person on a platter that we get to devour (Jn. 6:54-56). Our souls were fashioned to source from the living Word, being satisfied in him (Matt. 4:4).

The temptation of the devil is to shift our sourcing to the gift and what He gives instead of the gift and the giver. One is satisfaction in what the Lord gives and the other, satisfaction in the Lord himself. There is no question that we live in a culture that has money sitting preeminent as one of the primary promises that will satisfy our souls. The gospel that preaches "money will satisfy" is stealing away what only the preeminence of Jesus can give. Money isn't the root of all evil, the love of money is. The question can't become, "How much money can I have and still be devoted to God?" The question we each have to consider is, "How much money replaces my personal trust, faith, and satisfaction in God?" The moment money replaces Jesus' supremacy as the affectionate lover of our life is the moment we have made money preeminent rather than Christ. I promise that our greatest place of satisfaction is found when the affections of our heart have Christ sitting as supreme.

The Preeminence of Lust
For people will be lovers of pleasure rather than lovers of God.
2 Tim. 3:4

Lust is more than just an activity of the flesh, it is a worship war. This war of lust is primarily a place that is stealing away the pleasure people were meant to find in the preeminence of Christ. As stated in 2 Timothy, the increase of false pleasure will heighten in the last days creating the most idolatrous form of worship in human history. Satan's determination to lure the human heart away from worshipping Christ is increasing in the generation we find ourselves in. As a result, false forms of pleasure rooted in worship of self are being normalized to the point that it is considered cruel, judgmental, and hateful to preach holy pleasure found only in Christ.

There are many facets of Satan's tactics to steal away the preeminence of Christ by creating a false promise of pleasure found in worldly lust. The desire for intimate satisfaction is hardwired into every human being. Sex is one of the primary pleasures in which our desire for intimacy is fulfilled. Sex is a powerful dynamic of human relationship that God made for marriage. However, Satan is assaulting this blueprint of God's design. As a counterfeit option for satisfaction Satan is wooing the ache in our hearts for intimate pleasure, connection, and acceptance with lust for others outside of marriage. This is damaging to our soul, as sex is intended by God to be more than an exchange of pleasure, but a binding together of two beings. Sex is one of the primary places where transfer of emotional and spiritual intimacy occurs. Meaning, the emotional and spiritual facets of another person are shared with their sexual partner. This reality is remarkable and should help give us greater insight into why God designed sex to happen within marriage. His design for sex isn't meant to steal away pleasure; on the contrary, it is meant to protect and enhance pleasure within our lives.

Beyond merely sex, Satan's strategy to create lustful thoughts is his attempt to wage war against the affections of our heart intimately being satisfied in communion with Christ. The warfare of lust is more than just sexual perversion, it is a strategy to make our bodies experience pleasure outside of Christ. It is Satan's strategy to call us into communion with another bridegroom, lusting after lovers outside of Christ. This scheme of lusting after lovers other than Christ leaves us less satisfied than we were before our search for intimate pleasure.

Lust displaces the preeminence of Jesus as our primary pleasure. Our primary pleasure was meant to be in Christ Jesus himself, savoring him in our soul as we abide in and with the Holy Spirit. Truthfully, each of us is bowing down to an altar of something. The seduction to lust tempts us to bow down at the altar of pleasure and to place lust as the preeminent pursuit of our life. Rejecting this seductive scheme of Satan and pursuing passionately the pleasure found in life with Christ will cultivate in us the continual intimate satisfaction our souls are searching after.

The Preeminence of Alcohol

Therefore do not be foolish, but understand what the will of the Lord is. And do not get drunk with wine, for that is debauchery, but be filled with the Spirit.
Eph. 5:17-18

This area of warfare includes substances that sedate and fill the body with a pseudo joy and drunkenness. This area of warfare can quickly become legalistic as well. The point isn't whether alcohol is evil or not. But what we lean on is what we glean from. If we glean from alcohol to comfort us in times of trouble or deliver us from despair we will continually be left leaning in increasing measure on its substance to satisfy our lives. This is a dangerous precedent that can quickly be set in one's life. If not alert and sober to the spiritual realities of warfare occurring within the context of addictive substances, we may quickly fall into the trap of satisfying our souls with a substance that steals away Christ being the preeminent substance we search after.

Let me be clear, wine isn't the substance of evil, Satan is. On the contrary wine is described by David as a gift given by God (Ps. 104:15). But any good gift given by God that becomes the preeminent pleasure of our life, rather than Christ, produces death. When we take a gift like wine and make it the preeminent source for pleasure and alleviation from pain we have let a lesser lover come and occupy the space that is meant for Christ. Addictive substances like alcohol and drugs have an ability to produce a false reality, creating in people a false sense of joy, satisfaction, and gladness.

One of the primary exhortations given throughout the New Testament is for believers to be alert and of sober mind, so as to pray (1 Pet. 4:7). As is clearly stated in this passage, the saints were meant to understand the purposes of God, partnering with him to accomplish his will. The mind is being either conformed or transformed. Alcohol and addictive substances have a unique ability to conform our mind to the system of thinking that is in conflict with the will of God. Because the will of God is for us to have life to the fullest. When conformed to finding pleasure in the patterns and promises of the world, we have consequently surrendered satisfying our souls to the one whose will is to steal, kill, and destroy (Jn. 10:10). Whatever is filling the affections of our heart will affect our mind, either transforming it into the likeness of

Christs or conforming it to the patterns of the world (Rom. 12:2, 1 Cor. 2:16). For believers, one empowers us to pray and extract our pleasure from the preeminence of Christ while the other empowers us to extract our pleasure from the world, making its promises preeminent in our lives.

Debauchery is the byproduct of one fulfilling the affections of their heart with alcohol, while holiness is the byproduct of one's affections being fulfilled and filled with the Holy Spirit. There is hope for those that currently are entangled in filling and fulfilling their personal pleasure with the addictive substances discussed. Christ deeply desires to deliver us from the will of the one who steals, setting us free by the power of his preeminent presence filling our soul.

The Preeminence of Religion

"You search the Scriptures because you think that in them you have eternal life; and it is they that bear witness about me, yet you refuse to come to me that you may have life."
John 5:39-40

The preeminence of religion can quickly infiltrate the affections of our heart. This is often seductive in nature as it provides a form of godliness to the zealous passionate lovers of God but is void of him being the primary prize. Jesus identified this spirit, calling it the yeast of the Pharisees and Sadducees (Matt. 16:6). Throughout Jesus' life we can see how he continually confronts this spirit in the religious elite. There are many forms of warfare that keep people from fully embracing Christ, and one of them includes the yeast of religion that can quickly work its way into the affections of our heart.

The Pharisees' and Sadducees' pleasure came from religion not God. They made intellectual stimulation about God more important than God himself. This produced an experience with the traditions, concepts, philosophies, and doctrines related to God. It created a personal and collective culture that made these things about God higher than their loyalty to their King. Because of this, they were void of a life that bore the fruit of participating with God in that which they preached (Matt. 23:3). The very thing they so earnestly sought to satisfy their soul, they rejected because religion was preeminent in their lives over God.

While I am not attempting to bring condemnation, I am attempting to enlighten our hearts to see where this yeast may be working in the midst of our own lives. In the Church we can quickly cultivate a culture that has loyalty to our denominational tribe over dedication and loyalty to the supremacy of Christ. The issues between tribes often begin to divide those Jesus came to unify. If our methods of Church are preeminent in our worship styles, teaching methods, or Sunday services we will end up usurping the King's proper place in his people. We will create a form of godliness in our religious beliefs, traditions, and styles that preemptively trump Christ's supremacy.

Personally and collectively it is crucial that we watch over the loyalty to the culture we are creating. This requires an openness to believe that we may be letting the yeast of religious spirit work into the affections of our heart and admitting it is affecting the culture being created in our Church. Without letting the Spirit divide between the King and his Kingdom and the personal culture of Christianity that we have created in his name, we will unknowingly continue to create forms and systems about him that are void of him. When as a spiritual family our collective culture of the way we respond to the King and His Kingdom becomes the sign or baseline of ours and everybody else's devotion to Jesus we quickly become judgmental people who are wise in our own eyes. When our affiliation with the King is determined by the expression of the way we worship or the Christian culture we have created, we have replaced our affiliation with Christ based upon his powerful atonement with culturally created form, tradition, and expression.

Jesus is bringing every expression of Christianity into one tribe to unite us as one Church. The warfare around religion holds a significant impact on how the Church moves forward in her partnership with Christ in this age. Recognizing this warfare and extinguishing this spirit from our cultures empowers us to place the King and the culture of his Kingdom as first place in all things in the Church. It is within Christ sitting supreme over all things that the culture of our personal and collective lives reflect the Kingdom of God on earth as it is in heaven.

Greater the Problem, Greater the Provision

For we do not wrestle against flesh and blood, but against the rulers, against the authorities, against the cosmic powers over this present darkness, against the spiritual forces of evil in the heavenly places.
Eph. 6:12

Paul gives us the appropriate worldview, which is that we live in a battle zone and it is not a battle with flesh and blood but rather with dimensions of the spiritual realm. The cosmic war that is occurring exists within an unseen realm that is more eternally real than what you can see right in front of you. These demonic powers are primarily attempting to steal, kill, and destroy, preventing Jesus from receiving his reward of preeminence in all people and places. These spiritual forces are fighting to steal away the affections of our heart and keep them from being given to

Christ. In the same measure, hell hates our hearts feeling about humanity the way Jesus does. By stealing away the affections of our heart toward Christ, Satan consequently is stealing away the loving affections we were meant to have toward others. When we allow Satan to prevent us from loving others, the perceived war that we are waging becomes against the seen rather than the unseen. When this occurs we participate in a futile battle, boxing the wind aimlessly, attempting to win a fight, all the while being in the ring with the wrong opponent.

While this statement seems obvious we continue to fall into the scheme of Satan and the ways he desires to divide us in our hearts toward one another through gossip, slander, and hate. If we believe it to be true that our battle is never against flesh and blood, then we are set free for a lifestyle empowered by the love of God, no matter the hate that is being heaped on our lives from others. Within this personal revelation of warfare comes incredible freedom. When the actions of others no longer dictate our own actions we are free to live with no offense, bitterness, or unforgiveness.

Once we realize that the war at hand is unseen, we can become ambassadors of reconciliation in all situations and circumstances (2 Cor. 5:20). When properly positioned to wage war, we find that all battles are primarily for the purpose of setting us and others free through placing Christ as preeminent in the affections of our lives. It is within this realm of revelation that all problems that arise become opportunities for our partnership with God to break through demonic entanglements to set us and others free. Suddenly, the greater the problem that occurs because of the war being waged, the greater the promise we inherit through the provision God pours out as he delivers us from the devil's grasp, thrusting us into receiving his Son as supreme.

Therefore take up the whole armor of God, that you may be able to withstand in the evil day, and having done all, to stand firm.
Eph. 6:13

Understanding the armor with which we properly arm ourselves for this battle is crucial if we are going to wage war from a place of victory. In Christ we do not have to fight for victory rather we fight from victory. These are two very different places that determine the posture we take in seasons of warfare. One fights with an undetermined outcome while the other fights from a predetermined place of victory. Paul prophetically declares the outcome of warfare for those who are in Christ saying, "No, in all these things we are more than conquerors through him who loved us" (Rom. 8:37). Being more than a conqueror doesn't mean that a battle doesn't exist. It is impossible to conquer anything apart from a battle. On the contrary, being more than conqueror means that the outcome of the battle is predetermined, Yahweh God wins every single time. It is in this personal revelation that every place of warfare waged against us becomes an opportunity to conquer Satan's schemes by trusting in the preeminent power of Christ in us.

The purpose of the armor of God is centered on securing the supremacy and preeminence of Christ. Again, the primary activity of the enemy is to dethrone the supremacy of Jesus in people and places. Satan rages to make Jesus last place in the hearts of his people. Simply put, whether second place or last place, if not first place, Satan has accomplished his mission in stealing away Christ's supremacy. The armor of God not only comes out from being rooted in Christ, each piece of the armor of God is equally connected to the supremacy of Christ. Meaning that being fastened firmly in the armor of God is a result of Christ's presence not only dwelling in the wearer, but them continually surrendering to him. Being clothed in the armor of God isn't something we muster up in our own strength. Rather, it occurs as we choose daily to die to ourselves, and surrender to Christ's supremacy as Lord of our lives. When doing so, the armor of God is spiritually fastened around our form, protecting us against the schemes that attempt to steal away Christ being supreme in all things in our life.

Take the helmet of salvation…
Eph. 6:17

The helmet of salvation is clearly protecting our renewed mind given in Christ. Our new nature in Christ has renewed and continues to renew our mind to think from the spiritual reality of our salvation. Through the body and blood of Christ, we have been given a new mind to think in ways that are holy, blameless, and pure (1 Cor. 2:12, Eph. 4:23-24, Col. 1:21-22). This transformed mind can only continue to be renewed through a fixation and fascination with the supremacy of Christ, as that which we gaze at we become like (Col. 3:2, 2 Cor. 3:18). The helmet of salvation, given in the supremacy of Christ, empowers our mind to be protected from placing other thoughts preeminent over Christ. In Christ, our minds are meant to think from the reality of the full redemptive work of Jesus. No matter what warfare is being waged against our mind, the saints overcoming power occurs through abiding by faith in the stronghold of the full redemptive work of Jesus Christ. It is the helmet of salvation that secures Christ as supreme in our mind, renewing our thoughts to habitually think about and like Him.

Put on the breastplate of righteousness...
Eph. 6:14

The armor of God is purposed to empower and protect us to continually offer our lives to God and so inherit eternal life. Jesus declares this multiple times throughout the gospels, commissioning us to love the Lord our God with all our heart, soul, and mind (Matt. 22:37). While the helmet of salvation protects our ability to love God with our mind, the breastplate of righteousness protects the affections of our heart to seek first Christ and his righteousness (Matt. 6:33). The breastplate of righteousness protects our heart from letting in lesser lovers, securing Christ as the supreme lover of our lives. In Christ, our nature is to seek God by faith with righteousness and holiness. The breastplate of righteousness empowers our hearts to continue to operate in our new nature, consequently seeking the righteousness of God as the default of our life.

Stand therefore, having fastened on the belt of truth...
 Eph. 6:14

The belt of truth is what firmly establishes us in an eternal reality. While "truth(s)" are running around rampantly, the reality is that one truth is held as supreme above all other truths. The simplicity of that truth lies in the words of Jesus who says, "I am the way, the truth, and the life. No one comes to the Father except through me" (John 14:6). The ultimate truth of the universe is Christ, who is the wisdom and revelation of all truth. Truth is life and is manifested in the man Christ Jesus. When Jesus is the centerpiece of our reality, a powerful transformation of our being begins to take place by the hands of the Holy Spirit. Jesus becoming the reality of truth for our life breaks the rage of Satan and his attempts to steal, kill, and destroy. In truth we can all stand in the midst of Satan's lies, being fastened and focused on the supremacy of Christ.

As shoes for your feet, having put on the readiness given by the gospel of peace.
Eph. 6:15

This passage is referring to what is preeminent over the movements of our lives, as all of us are moving to accomplish a mission. While the world attempts to ready our feet with its false sense of purpose, the gospel of peace empowers us to passionately partner with God by faith to accomplish his will in and through our lives. Readying our feet with the gospel of peace empowers us to partner with God's purposes, zealously following him.

Walking in the shoes of the Spirit personally produces confidence that we walk in peace with God through the life of Christ. This gospel of peace isn't merely intellectually understood, it is a spiritual reality that transforms us to live in constant communion with God. This communion affects every movement we make with God, allowing us to stay in step with him moment by moment. The armor of shoes readies all our movements to inwardly carry the gospel of peace for the purpose of outwardly manifesting its realities. Paul gives revelation of this mission stating, "God gave us the ministry of reconciliation ... Therefore, we are ambassadors for Christ, God making his appeal through us. We implore you on behalf of Christ, be reconciled to God" (2 Cor. 5:18, 20). What a mission we have been adopted to co-labor in, carrying the living gospel of peace that reconciles man with God. Christ sitting supreme in our lives manifests into a moving mandate, that creates a lifestyle whose primary purpose is the advancement of the Kingdom of God.

In all circumstances take up the shield of faith, with which you can
extinguish all the flaming darts of the evil one.
Eph. 6:16

This is one of the most intense descriptions of what this particular armor accomplishes in our lives. Our faith in the preeminent power of Christ extinguishes all of Satan's fiery arrows thrown our way. It is our faith that develops our belief of truth, and thus is a weapon of warfare that extinguishes the enemy and embraces the power of Christ in battle.

Faith is ultimately expressed through what we believe. Everyone on the earth is believing in something. Whether Christian or atheist, each person is putting faith in what they believe to be true, moving forward to follow something. The ultimate truth produces in us firm faith in the supremacy of Christ, moving forward in life with our Father in Heaven. Moving in life apart from faith in our Father produces actions that are devised by the devil and disobedient to God (Rom. 14:23, Heb. 11:6). Having Christ Jesus at the center of our faith is an act of war that blocks the fiery arrows of the enemy attempting to burn down our lives and instead, enables us to live faithfully for God.

Take up the sword of the Spirit, which is the word of God, praying at all
times in the Spirit, with all prayer and supplication.
Eph. 6:17-18

The sword which slays Satan's schemes—set up against the supremacy of Christ in our lives—is the word of God. The Word of

God that pierced through the dominion of darkness at the beginning of time and then was made manifest two thousand years ago is the man Christ Jesus (Jn. 1:1-3, 1:14). The Word of God is not merely words written on a page but the name of the man by whom the world was created and for and by whom it is held together (Col. 1:16).

The sword of the Spirit comes to destroy the tactics of the devil and to set us free into life in the Son of God. While this sword can be swung from our hands on behalf of ourselves and others, the mightiest warrior is swinging this sword on our behalf to demolish Satan's schemes that attempt to steal away our ability to live free in the Spirit. Though painful for a moment, if surrendered to, the Word of God that is sharper than any double-edged sword will separate the schemes that set themselves up against our freedom (Heb. 4:12). Letting the sword of the Spirit pierce our flesh comes as a result of submitting to the discipline of the Lord who judges the attitudes and thoughts of our hearts. This division of soul and spirit will progressively remove Satan's manipulation in our lives.

The sword of the Spirit is a divine weapon that demolishes strongholds. Though in the world, the weapons we fight with are contrary to what the world wields in days of battle (2 Cor. 10:3). The Word of God is at the right hand of the Father making war through intercession on behalf of humanity (Rom. 8:34). Swinging the sword of the Spirit to slay the strongholds of Satan comes through the divine weapon of warfare, prayer. The Word of God births in us that which is in him. Meaning, in the Spirit we can partner with the intercessory prayer and supplications of Jesus. The reason prayer and supplication are mentioned immediately after describing the most proactive weapon of warfare is because they are the most powerful and effective weapons we wield for victory. Prayer postures us in communion with God, by faith depending on his will, asking for his provision, and declaring his victory.

When we get the Word of God in our mouth and apply and pray it in all circumstances in life, we consequently, by faith, place Christ preeminent in all we do. Relying on the Word of God for our provision will create, in our hearts, houses of prayer both personally and collectively, consequently partnering with God to drive out the darkness of the devil.

Jesus demonstrated the effectiveness of this weapon as the words of God were his personal protection against deception as well as the sword with which to overcome Satan in the desert with (Matt. 4:2-3, 5-6). Jesus combatted the deception of the devil that attempted to steal away his obedience to God by depending on and declaring his Father's word. These words continue to be a source of victory that are active, living, breathing, and alive (Heb. 4:12). When his words are stored in our heart and supreme in our life, then we are positioned to bring assault on the kingdom of darkness (Ps. 119:11). We block with our faith the fiery arrows of the devil, but we engage his dominion with the Word of God.

The horse is made ready for the day of battle, but the victory belongs to the Lord.
Prov. 21:31

While it is critical to prepare for days of battle by daily putting on the armor of God, there is an ultimate principle that we partake in for definitive victory. Solomon gives us a glimpse into the wisdom of reigning in battle saying, "The horse is made ready for the day of battle but the victory belongs to the Lord" (Prov. 21:31). It isn't that we don't make the necessary preparations, wisely walking in the strategies of the Lord. However, the final declaration that delivers us from the devil is the victory given through the blood and body of Christ on the cross (Col. 2:15). There are seasons where the warfare becomes so heavy that though we have properly prepared, we feel as if there isn't an ounce of strength in us to wield our weapons. It is on these days that though we can't fight in strength, we stand in weakness, firmly standing in our faith knowing that our victory belongs to the Lord. When weakly standing in confident faith, everything set against the intimate knowledge of God is forced to flee, freeing us from our spiritual oppression. Our faith to stand ushers in the mighty man of war, who with zealous passion raises a battle cry, triumphing over all enemies that seek to supplant and suppress his supremacy (Is. 42:13).

In the Final Analysis

This book is a meager attempt to make the central point that the warp and woof of our faith is the supremacy of Christ. All of the Spirit's work, the scriptures revelation, and satan's opposition are focused on this glorious issue. The meaning of our lives, relationships, mission, and all other things are wrapped up in the preeminence of Jesus.

So, in conclusion, I invite you to set your hearts and minds upon the great issue of the universe which simply put is the first-placeness of Jesus Christ in all things. He will be first in all nations. He will be first in all creation. He will be first in the hearts of the eternal sons and daughters of God. This is where all of time is headed, so I encourage you to get a head start!

At the center of my prayers for you, as well as the Lord's beloved Church, is that you would receive the zealous work of the Holy Spirit which is always working toward filling all things with Christ. You can be utterly confident that the broken idolatrous nations of this present age will be fully satiated with his glory and government in the age to come. They will submit and sing to the King of the ages as sure as the sun will rise after a long dark night.

The supremacy of Christ filling all things will alone bring about his full glory and our deepest satisfaction. This will all reach its climax at the return of our Savior King. Maranatha!

Made in United States
Orlando, FL
05 May 2022

17541362R00068